How to Democratize the European Union . . . and Why Bother?

Philippe C. Schmitter

ROWMAN & LITTLEFIELD PUBLISHERS, INC.
Lanham • Boulder • New York • Oxford

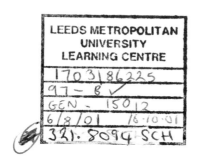
ROWMAN & LITTLEFIELD PUBLISHERS, INC.

Published in the United States of America
by Rowman & Littlefield Publishers, Inc.
4720 Boston Way, Lanham, Maryland 20706
http://www.rowmanlittlefield.com

12 Hid's Copse Road
Cumnor Hill, Oxford OX2 9JJ, England

British Library Cataloguing in Publication Information Available

Library of Congress Cataloging-in-Publication Data

Schmitter, Philippe C.
   How to democratize the European Union—and why bother? / Philippe C. Schmitter.
   p. cm. — (Governance in Europe)
   Includes bibliographical references and index.
   ISBN 0-8476-9904-8 (cloth) —ISBN 0-8476-9905-6 (paper)
   1. European Union. 2. Democratization—European Union countries. I. Title. II. Series.

JN30.S344 2000
341.242'2—dc21   99-053003

Printed in the United States of America

∞™ The paper used in this publication meets the minimum requirements of
American National Standard for Information Sciences—Permanence of Paper
for Printed Library Materials, ANSI/NISO Z39.48–1992.

Contents

Preface

This is a relatively short book, but it has had a long trajectory. It began when I was fortunate enough to have been invited to be a visiting professor at the Centro de Estudios Avanzados en Ciencias Sociales of the Instituto Juan March during the spring of 1996—for which I wish to thank its codirectors, José Maria Maravall and José Ramon Montero. In the institute's splendid facilities, I got the idea that it might be fruitful if I tried to combine two seemingly disparate research interests: democratization at the national level and integration at the European level. Thanks to its very competent and helpful staff, especially Marta Peach and Jackie de la Fuente, and the stimulus provided by the doctoral students in my seminar "The Theory and Practice of European Integration," I produced a first draft of this manuscript that I presented in a series of public lectures in Madrid. While I cannot claim that these lectures were an instant hit, they did help me to recruit José Ignacio Torreblanca, who subsequently worked with me on the decision-making scheme that is presented here in revised form in chapter 4.

After a brief interval at Stanford University, I accepted a position at the European University Institute (EUI), where I found just the right atmosphere among its faculty, staff, and *ricercatori* to pursue the matter further. In seminars at the *Badia* overlooking Florence, I was literally inundated with helpful criticisms and suggestions. The presence there of the Centre Robert Schumann was important in encouraging me to develop further the more praxis-oriented and reformist aspects of the manuscript, especially my thoughts on the issue of constitutionalization in chapter 5. Eva Breivik was her usual helpful self and even put up with several hysterical struggles between me and my computer. More often than not, it was Bernard Gbikpi who managed to get me untangled—and who did a great deal to polish up the final footnotes and bibliography. Ian Gough and the other participants in the European Forum on "The Future of the Welfare State"

(1998–99) provided some very useful criticism of my initial thoughts concerning a possible extension of social citizenship to the European Union that are presented in the excursus at the end of chapter 2.

Bits and pieces of various versions of this manuscript have been discussed before many other audiences, including the Cellule de Prospective of the European Commission, where it received a polite but reserved reception. One of the participants came up to me afterward with a horrified look on his face and asked, "Do you know what you have done with that voting scheme of yours?" I, of course, said, "No. What have I inadvertently done?" "Reinvented the Holy Roman Empire!" was his answer. Subsequent research on my part has revealed that he was (partially) correct.

These exchanges and those I have constantly had with colleagues and students at the EUI have, no doubt, improved the quality of the final product. Especially, they have helped me to anticipate many of the difficulties and objections that even the "modest reforms" I propose are bound to generate. As Machiavelli once said:

> There is nothing more difficult to execute, nor more dubious of success, nor more dangerous to administer, than to introduce a new system of things: for he who introduces it has all those who profit from the old system as his enemies and he has only lukewarm allies in all those who might profit from the new system. (*The Prince*, VI, 94)

I cannot claim that all of my suggestions for reforming a more democratic European Union will be equally compelling or likely to be taken seriously. No doubt, many will be dismissed by both those defending the old order and those not yet confident that a new one is possible. My (self-assigned) task has been to provoke as wide-ranging a debate as possible on an issue that has just begun to receive the attention it deserves.

I cannot thank each of those who helped me in this task individually. The list would be too long, but they know who they are, and some may even be able to spot exactly the passages where their contributions were registered. One person, however, is all over the book, even though we have rarely discussed it explicitly since it lies outside her usual wide range of interests: Terry Karl, my intellectual *camarade de longue date*.

I also absolve everyone but myself for any responsibility for the errors and omissions that inevitably remain.

1

Euro-democracy: Introduction

My intention in this book is to explore the possibility and the desirability of democratizing the European Union (EU). In this chapter, I analyze the EU as an emerging polity with certain distinctive features when contrasted with the existing nation-states that are its members. Its status as a "nonstate" and a "nonnation" poses some very challenging problems with regard to its eventual democratization. Should this ever be seriously attempted, I argue, it will be necessary to reinvent the key institutions of modern political democracy: citizenship, representation, and decision making. In chapters 2, 3, and 4, I suggest what some of these "reinventions" might be in the form of modest proposals for reform in each of these three dimensions. For it is my conviction that the EU has neither the political will nor the functional necessity to democratize itself *tutto e subito*—completely and immediately. The only feasible strategy is to apply the method that Jean Monnet used to initiate Europe's economic integration in the 1950s to its political integration in the first decades of the twenty-first century. One has to start with *petits pas* and exploit them incrementally to produce *grands effets*. Moreover, under present conditions and foreseeable future scenarios, there will be no widespread and spontaneous pressure to do so from below. The initiative for regime change in the EU has to come from above or from within—that is, from its member states or its internal institutions. Finally, in chapter 5, I take up the issue of "Why bother?" and, especially, "Why bother now?" Given the manifest absence of a widespread desire on the part of Europeans for "Euro-democracy" and the equally obvious reluctance of the Eurocrats in Brussels to take such a risk, why is it so imperative to begin the process of democratization soon? Part of the answer I find in the imperatives likely to be generated in the near future by eastern enlargement and monetary unification. The rest I find in the need for the process of European integration to replace its exhausted strategy of exploiting economic interdependencies with a new one of generating transnational political alliances and loyalties.

WHAT SHOULD ONE ASSUME ABOUT DEMOCRACY IN THE EUROPEAN UNION?

Like any student approaching the complex *objet politique nonidentifié* that is the European Union, I began with certain assumptions that pervasively influenced my analysis. I am convinced that they are plausible but admit that I would be hard-pressed to prove any of them. If they do seem implausible to the reader, I urge him or her not to read further since all of my subsequent argumentation is contingent upon their veracity.

1. The emerging Euro-polity has not yet acquired its definitive institutional configuration, either in terms of its territorial scale, its functional scope or its level of political authority.[1]
2. The Euro-polity in its present, provisional configuration is not a democracy and will not become one unless and until its member states decide explicitly to endow it with new rules and rights.[2]
3. The conjunctural forces affecting the Euro-polity's configuration are currently pushing the Euro-polity in contrary directions toward diverse outcomes, with no stable equilibrium likely to emerge in the near future.[3]
4. Nevertheless, its most likely outcome within the medium term (say, twenty years) is a form of nonstate, nonnational polity or stable political order that is novel—that is, will not resemble either an intergovernmental organization or a supranational state or any of the possible points along this institutional continuum.[4]
5. If, eventually, its member states decide to transform this novel polity into a democracy, they will have to experiment with new forms of citizenship, representation, and decision making in order to be successful. Merely copying the institutions of existing national democracies, even federal ones, will not suffice—and could even have counterproductive effects.[5]
6. No matter how reluctant they may be and how ill informed about what to do, the member states of the Euro-polity will eventually have to democratize it or risk losing what they have already attained (i.e., a high level of economic interdependence and a reliable degree of security community) through declining legitimacy with mass publics.[6]

WHAT WOULD A EURO-DEMOCRACY HAVE TO HAVE?

In principle, an eventual Euro-democracy would have to satisfy the generic characteristics of any modern political democracy, which Terry Karl and I have defined elsewhere as "a regime or system of governance in which rulers are held accountable for their actions in the public realm by citizens, acting indirectly through the competition and cooperation of their representatives."[7]

Note that, according to this definition, democracy does not consist of any particular configuration of institutions and is not confined to any specific level of aggregation. Accountability can take many different forms, even if regular "free and fair" elections between competing political parties has long been regarded as the most salient one. It is a property that emerges from the relationship of three distinctive sets of actors, regardless of their size, scale, or scope: rulers, citizens, and representatives.

Let us examine briefly each of the concepts in the prior definition in terms of the present practices of the European Union.[8]

1. A regime (or system of governance) is an ensemble of patterns that determines (a) the forms and channels of access to principal governmental positions, (b) the characteristics of the actors who are admitted to or excluded from such access, (c) the resources or strategies that these actors can use to gain access, and (d) the rules that are followed in the making of publicly binding decisions. To produce its effect, the ensemble must be institutionalized; that is, the various patterns must be habitually known, practiced, and accepted by most, if not all, of the actors. Increasingly, this has involved their explicit legalization or constitutionalization, but many very stable regime norms can have an implicit, informal, prudential, or precedential basis.

By these criteria, the EU is definitely a regime, although not a democratic one. The characteristics of the actors (i.e., citizens) who are permitted direct access to its institution are not fully defined (or contingent upon specifications established by its national member states), and the absence of an explicitly constitutional bill of rights means that which resources or strategies are legitimate is also largely defined at the national level or left to the vagaries of practice at the supranational level. Finally, the modifications embedded in the Single European Act (SEA), the Maastricht Treaty on European Union (TEU), and the Amsterdam Treaty concerning qualified majority voting do not constitute a definitive statement of the decision rules that actors expect to live with for the indefinite future.

2. The rulers are those who occupy dominant positions in the formal
   structure of governance. Democracies are not anarchies. They are
   not voluntarily or spontaneously coordinated but depend on the presence of persons who occupy specialized roles and can give legitimate commands to others. What distinguishes democratic rulers
   from nondemocratic ones are the norms that determine how they become rulers and the practices that hold them accountable for what
   they do once they have become rulers.

Here, the key issue is whether the supranational authorities of the EU
have sufficient capacity for giving direct commands legitimately and effectively. Not only are there relatively few Eurocrats and not only do they
dispose of vastly less resources than the rulers of their member states, but
also they devote most of their effort to giving commands to these national
rulers who remain directly responsible for the actual acts of governance.
As the mounting complaints testify, the compliance of these more numerous and more resourceful authorities at the national and subnational levels cannot be taken for granted.

Moreover, the EU's rulers are only accountable en bloc to the directly
elected representatives of citizens. They cannot be refused or dismissed
as individuals responsible for specific tasks. Although the data are not
clearly apposite, the public opinion surveys of Eurobaromètre do suggest
that most of the EU's subjects/citizens do not feel directly obligated by
or identified with its commands, and they have increasingly raised serious doubts about the legitimacy of some of its highly secretive and technically obscure decision-making practices. Finally, the opt-out, opt-in
provisions of several EU policy arenas (e.g., the European monetary system and the Schengen Agreement on cooperation in police and internal
security affairs) and the subsequent sanctification of this sort of variable
geometry in several clauses of the TEU would seem to indicate that countries (and hence their citizens) that do not agree with certain measures
will not necessarily be bound by the decision of the majority — whether
qualified or not.

3. The public realm involves that part of the collective choice process
   in which norms binding on the society as a whole and backed by the
   coercive force of the state are made. This realm can vary a great deal
   across democracies depending on how previous decisions have
   drawn distinctions between the public and the private, between state
   and society, between legitimate coercion and voluntary exchange,
   between collective needs and individual preferences. Differences of
   opinion over the optimal mix of the two provide much of the substantive content of political conflict within established democracies.

There is no question that these issues involved in delimiting the public realm have been debated extensively in the EU, but they have not been resolved. The notion that the Single European Act of 1985–86 had definitively opted for a narrowly "liberal" conception has been denied by subsequent developments. While its nature has changed substantially, regulation of economic exchanges has increased, not decreased, with the implementation of the SEA. Pace the provision of regional funds, however, the arrangement has yet to engage in any substantial and deliberate redistribution of funds within its class and territorial borders, other than the sectoral welfare state it has created for agriculture.

4. Citizens provide the most distinctive element in democratic regimes. All types of regimes have rulers of some sort and a public realm of some dimension; only democracies have citizens *strictu sensu.*

The EU has only just begun to specify the distinctive rights and obligations of its individual citizens, and, so far, they are far inferior in quality and quantity to those defined and protected by its national member states. Nevertheless, the Treaty of European Union signed at Maastricht in 1992 formally specifies in its Articles 8, 8a, 8b, 8c, 8d, and 8e a set of rights, involving such items as (1) the enfranchisement of residents of other EU member states to vote and run as candidates in local elections, which could be the first step in extending the right to all Euro-citizens to vote in all elections in the constituencies where they permanently reside regardless of their national citizenship; (2) the reaffirmation of the rights of all individuals, nationals and resident foreigners, to petition the European Parliament (EP); (3) the creation of an ombudsman's office at the EU level; and (4) a pledge to make the proceedings of EU institutions more "transparent" in the future. The last of these articles (8e) even invites the Council of Ministers "acting unanimously" and only on a proposal from the commission and after consulation with the European Parliament to strengthen or to add to this list in the future.

When one combines these newly founded aspects of political citizenship with the "four freedoms" of economic citizenship already promised by the Single European Act of 1986—that is, free movement of trade, capital, services, and persons—one has the potential basis for the development of a varied and consequential "Euro-citizenship" above and beyond existing national citizenships guaranteed by its member states.

It should be noted, however, that Euro-citizenship differs in one fundamental aspect from national citizenship. While it conveys equal rights and opportunities upon individuals, their collective political weight in EU decision making is highly unequal, given the complex formulae that systematically give the smaller countries more seats in the EP and votes in the Council of Ministers. Moreover, its exercise is relatively marginal, given the weakness of the EP in the decision-making process as a whole. Granted that overrepresentation of rural districts and other peculiarities of malapportionment and gerrymandering are never completely absent from national democracies, the EU's weightings across member states is of a qualitatively different magnitude. It could also be argued that national parliaments have lost influence relative to other decision-making bodies within national polities, but the EP has never had much influence to lose.

5. Competition has not always been considered an essential defining condition of democracy, although at least since the *Federalist Papers* it has become widely accepted that competition among more or less permanent "factions" is a "necessary evil" of all democracies that operate on a more than local scale.

   The most widely diffused conception of this competition makes it virtually synonymous with the presence of regular, fairly conducted, and honestly counted elections of uncertain outcome. Without denying their centrality for democracy, these contests between candidates are held sporadically and only allow citizens to choose between the highly aggregated alternatives offered by political parties. In between, however, individuals can compete to influence public policy through a wide variety of other intermediaries: interest associations, social movements, locality groupings, clientelistic arrangements, and so forth. Modern democracy, in other words, offers a variety of competitive processes and channels for the expression of interests—associational as well as partisan, functional as well as territorial, collective as well as individual. All are integral to its practice.

   Nor is there agreement on the appropriate rules of competition. There is certainly a commonly accepted image of democracy that identifies it exclusively with the principle of rule by the majority. The problem, however, arises when sheer numbers meet special intensities, when a perfectly properly assembled majority (especially a stable majority) produces decisions that negatively affect some minority (especially a threatened cultural or ethnic minority). Another way of putting this intrinsic tension between numbers and intensities would be to say that in modern democracies, votes may be counted, but influences are also weighted—carefully.

On these grounds, the democratic status of the EU is ambiguous. Partisan competition is recognized and enshrined in the elections to the EP and in its internal legislative operations—even if the lines of cleavage and aggregation are often inconsistent from country to country and change frequently at the European level.[9] Voters in Euro-elections are simply not offered an opportunity to choose between rival partisan elites presenting alternative programs at that level of aggregation. In any event, this principle of party-structured competition does not govern the formation of the commission or its policy deliberations. Nomination by national governments according to fixed quotas prevails, and those who are subsequently appointed are explicitly not supposed to represent the interests of their respective governments. Most important, there is virtually no way that individual citizens voting in free, equal, fair, and competitive Euro-elections could influence the composition of Euro-authorities, much less bring about a rotation of those in office.

Votes are taken by simple majority in the EP, but they are not generally binding or determinant, even if they have been increased in importance through the codecision procedures introduced by the TEU. It remains impossible to translate a majority produced by the European electorate at large into an effective and predictable change in government or policy. The best one can expect is an indirect expression through a qualified majority of the member states, which themselves all have majoritarian governments—at least on that range of issues that is subject to this decision rule. The closest analogy might be to imagine German democracy functioning only with the *Bundesrat* and no *Bundestag*.

Otherwise, the EU is a rather extreme case of a type of emerging democracy that stresses the weighting of intensities over the counting of votes, especially when those intensities are aggregated and expressed as "national interests." Not only are small countries overweighted in the voting formula of the Council of Ministers, but on a wide range of important issues unanimity is still required. As we shall see in chapter 4, the new codecision procedures between the council and the European Parliament prefigure a system of concurrent majorities. However, the absence of statutory guarantees for the powers of national, provincial, and/or local governments—pace the recent references to subsidiarity—means that a federalist consensus on the distribution of powers has not yet been established. One could describe the process of forming the commission as a sort of consociational arrangement in that all member states are included in a Grand Coalition, and, by tradition, those with more than one commissioner have tended to nominate them from opposing domestic parties.

Repeated efforts by the Eurocracy (and, most recently, by the presidents of the European Commission, Jacques Delors and Jacques Santer) to create a viable "social dialogue" among capital, labor, and themselves have yet to produce any regularized channeling of class-based interest intensities. The advisory Economic and Social Council has never made a serious contribution since its founding in the late 1950s.

Supplementing the institutionalized expression of national—and hence allegedly majoritarian—interests through the Council of Ministers is the less visible but nonetheless pervasive expression of minority interests through interest associations. From its founding, the Eurocracy has attracted (and occasionally sponsored) organizations representing specialized class, sectoral, and professional interests. Especially since the SEA, Brussels has been literally invaded by an increasing variety of "Euro-lobbies"—not just formal interest associations, but also social movements, individual enterprises, and law firms. While all this is entirely appropriate for a modern democracy, the normative issue is whether these channels are freely and fairly available to all social and economic groups, especially to minorities with intensive preferences. So far, the evidence suggests a mobilization of bias in favor of business and systemic problems in adjusting to the expanded scale of genuinely European interaction.

   6. Cooperation has always been a central feature of democracies. Actors must combine with each other by some voluntary process to make collective decisions binding on the polity as a whole. Most obviously, they must cooperate in order to compete. They must be capable of engaging in collective action through parties, associations, and movements that can select candidates, articulate preferences, petition authorities, and influence policies.
      But beyond this unavoidably "adversarial" aspect to democracy, its freedoms should encourage citizens to deliberate among themselves, discover their common needs, and resolve their possible conflicts without relying on centralized political authority. The "classical" conception of democracy stressed these qualities, and they are by no means extinct—despite repeated efforts by contemporary theorists to stress the analogy with behavior in the economic marketplace and to reduce all its operations to competitive interest maximization.[10]

As mentioned earlier, no viable party system has yet emerged at the level of the European Community/Union as a whole. To a limited extent, members of national parties do cooperate under supranational labels within the legislative process of the EP, but candidates for Euro-deputy are neither nominated nor funded through supranational parties. On the contrary, their selection by national party oligarchies and election by proportional representation, often within a single national constituency (except for Great Britain, with its traditional first-past-the-post individual constituencies), more or less ensure that the winning candidates will be unknown to the citizens who have elected them. In any case, none of this effort at partisan cooperation has been translated into cooperation in the formation of governing coalitions or cabinets.

Moreover, the sheer scale of the Euro-polity—not to mention its potpourri of languages and political traditions—seems to have inhibited the sort of deliberation among individual citizens that Tocqueville regarded as so crucial. With the exception of academic cooperation and the proliferation of policy centers and think tanks, there are very few sites outside EU institutions themselves at which Europe's practices and purposes can be discussed. During the difficulties that surrounded the ratification of the TEU, this sense of alienation from Brussels became manifest. Individuals proved willing to accept almost any rumor presented to them about arbitrary behavior on the part of Eurocrats—in large part because they were ill informed and unable to discuss these issues reasonably with their peers.

7. The principal agents of modern political democracy are representatives. Citizens may elect them or choose to support the parties, associations, or movements they lead, but representatives do the real business of governing. Moreover, most of these persons are not amateurs but professionals. Without individuals who invest in democracy to the extent that they orient their life's career around the aspiration to fill its key roles, it is doubtful that any democracy could survive. The central question is not whether there will be a "political elite" or even a "political class" but how that group of representatives will be composed and subsequently held accountable for its actions.

The EU is indeed surrounded by representatives, but these are hardly representative of the citizenry as a whole. At the functional level, they are overwhelmingly skewed to favor business interests. With the increased importance of the EP, there is some evidence of a shift of attention and greater access for social movements, consumer groups, and environmental constituencies, but they have a long way to go before they have redressed the imbalance. At the territorial level, representatives owe their allegiance almost exclusively to national constituencies. Recently, the TEU officially opened up an opportunity for the representation of subnational polities with the creation of an advisory Committee of Regions, but this may have no more effect than the preceding establishment of an Economic and Social Council.

What is missing are the *professional politicians* who represent transnational interests and passions. With the exception of the relatively unknown Eurocrats who labor away in its core bureaucracy, there are few persons who identify exclusively with the Euro-Polity. The careers of the politicians-cum-technicians who are momentarily active in its commission or who are elected to its parliament continue to be much more affected by what is happening in their countries of origin. Very few lose an election or fail to gain a promotion for something they have done in Brussels or Strasbourg, and many are sent there after their real careers are over. The composition of Europe's emerging "political class" may be more varied and

less predictable than that of its component parts, but it is much less coherent and capable of defending its distinctive practices and purposes.

*   *   *

Simplifying considerably, an eventual Euro-democracy would have to
be a regime with a public realm of its own in which citizens from the
polity as a whole would have to be capable of ensuring the accountability—via the competition and cooperation of their political representatives—of those rulers entitled to make and implement those decisions
that are binding on all members of that polity. This presents us with three
key sets of actors: citizens, representatives, and rulers whose behavior
has to be regularly and reliably patterned in such a way that accountability is ensured.[11]

In most modern settings, the regularity and reliability of these relation-
ships requires that they be (at least in part) protected by formal legal
norms. Given both the nature of the contracting parties and the process
whereby their bargaining over these norms takes place, it is highly likely
that this would eventually have to involve the negotiating, drafting, and
ratifying of a treaty instituting an explicit European constitution.[12] Which
is not to say that progress toward democratizing the Euro-polity has to
await this sort of "big bang" founding event. Many things could be done
less auspiciously and less controversially to improve its accountability to
the Euro-citizenry—as we shall see in subsequent chapters and in the excursus on constitutionalization.

WHAT DILEMMAS WOULD A EURO-DEMOCRACY HAVE TO FACE?

But let us first take a quick look at several difficult choices—dilemmas, if
you will—that would have to be resolved during the process of democratizing and eventually constitutionalizing the Euro-polity.

First, let us set aside the usual convenient "theoretical" devices for con-
stituting an acceptable democratic polity.[13] No impartial outside *législa-
teur* is going to appear providentially and produce a solution based on
such compelling abstract principles that the design of the Euro-democracy
will be recognized by all as an obvious emanation of the "General Will of
Europe." No charismatic leader is likely to so mesmerize the diverse populations of Europe that they will enthusiastically welcome his or her message and routinize it into a new set of magically legitimated institutions.[14]
No opaque "veil of ignorance" is going to descend and obscure the vision
that actors have of how various configurations of scale, scope, and procedures will affect their self-interest. No extraordinary "window of opportunity" is likely to open that will allow the participants to suspend their

mundane concerns with "low politics"—to be superseded by a unified devotion to the "high politics" of meta–rule making. No *Herrschaftsfreidiskurs* or "perfect speech situation" awaits those who would dare to produce a fair set of procedures and rights for the citizens of Europe.

If and when the Euro-polity gets down seriously to the task of filling its democracy deficit, it will be a much messier affair with a rather more prosaic purpose. These *pouvoirs constituents* (N.B. the plural) will not deliberate learnedly and try to persuade each other intellectually in the manner of the famous founding fathers of the United States.[15] They will negotiate under considerable public scrutiny and haggle their way to a mutually acceptable set of rules that will (hopefully) increase the accountability of rulers to citizens via representatives. Moreover, they will only be founding a regime—not a polity or, least of all, a nation. For better or worse (and admittedly on a much smaller scale), "Europe" was founded as a polity in 1957 at Messina. "Europe" as a nation has yet to appear, and no treaty or constitution is going to establish it *ex ante*. At best, it can only emerge *ex post*.

Moreover, whatever "refounding" of this polity occurred at Maastricht or Amsterdam (and might occur again in the near future), it is highly unlikely that such actions will definitively fix the external limits or establish the overriding identity of those involved. The eventual Euro-constituents will be asked to design a democratic regime for a territory and a citizenry whose future boundaries and identities are unknown.

If and when this daunting task is attempted, the participants are going to have to resolve some rather formidable practical dilemmas in the process—without the help of any enlightened outside leverage or very much reasoned inside deliberation. Two of these dilemmas are generic to the consolidation of democracy in any context;[16] two are more specific to the difficult choices that will have to be made within Europe.

First, the consolidation or constitutionalization of democracy involves resolving a complex double game in which politicians/representatives must first reach agreement on a viable set of rules for cooperation and competition among themselves and, then, convince the relevant citizenry that these rules are fair and appropriate for rendering rulers accountable. The challenge for democratic *constituents*, therefore, is to find a set of institutions that embody contingent consent among politicians—that is, that are regarded as fair and feasible among the principal players and are capable of invoking the eventual assent of citizens (i.e., are considered as legitimate by their followers-cum-audiences). Even if both groups do not necessarily have to agree on a set of goals or substantive policies that command widespread consensus at the same time, it may still be difficult to find mutually acceptable procedures. Not only are the choices *intrinsically conflictual*—with politicians grouped into different parties preferring rules that will best ensure their own reelection or eventual access to office, and citizens aggregated into different social groups wanting rules that will best ensure the accountability of their representatives—but they are also *extrinsically consequential*. Once they are translated via the uncertainties of elections and influence processes into governments that begin to produce public policies, the rules and practices applied will affect rates of economic growth, willingness to invest, variation in the value of currency, competitiveness in foreign markets, access to education, perceptions of cultural deprivation, racial balance, and even national identity. To make things worse, even if these substantive matters are not explicitly embedded in the initial constituent agreement, they will be anticipated by the actors involved and incorporated in the compromises they are willing to make with regard to specific rights and procedures.

Fortunately, this basic "democratic bargain," to use Robert Dahl's apt expression,[17] can vary a good deal from one society to another, depending on objective inequalities and cleavage patterns, as well as such subjective factors as the degree of mutual trust, the standard of fairness, the willingness to compromise, and the cultural legitimacy of different decision rules.

In the case of a prospective Euro-democracy, however, there are two quite serious further complications:

1. The politicians involved at the European level are much more entrenched (and, in the contemporary context, vastly more professionalized) within their respective national systems. Hence, they have greater resources and higher incentives to resist any possible threats to their tenure or reelectability than do the politicians involved in consolidating democracy in post-1974 neodemocracies.

2. The citizens potentially involved are much more confident of their rights and entitlements at the national level and much less conscious of their identities at the supranational level. They are also vastly less articulate and organized at the later level. Hence, they are going to be more difficult to sell on a new system of accountability (and there is potentially much less to offer them) than were the citizens of neodemocracies in Southern/Eastern Europe and South/Central America—and, even if they were to become aware of its advantages, they would be much less capable of pressing for them.

Both features strongly suggest that playing the double game of consolidation/ constitutionalization will not be easy for those who would democratize the Euro-polity. The temptation to settle for a restrictive, mutually beneficial arrangement among politicians who "in the national interest" would discriminate against an uncertain and unconscious Euro-citizenry seems almost irresistible. Moreover, it is unavoidable that the first steps in this direction will have to be gradual, cautious and "retractable." Whether such *petits pas* will be sufficient to contain the rising doubts about the legitimacy of the present decision-making procedures remains to be seen.

The second dilemma in democratizing the Euro-polity may be described as follows. Support for democracy (at whatever level of aggregation) is based on popular expectations for an improvement in existing conditions, usually, in the direction of greater equality; yet the successful consolidation of such a regime requires that politicians pay attention in its design to existing inequalities if they are to avoid significant defections or alienation of particular minorities.

Everywhere, this translates into a struggle over the rules between haves and have-nots and, more specifically, between the mobilization of majorities and the protection of minorities (between numbers and intensities in my jargon). Again, Europe adds some significant complications beyond the obvious likelihood that, given its size and diversity, the heterogeneity of preferences and tolerances for inequality is very great to begin with:

1. The existing pattern of inequalities to be addressed by an emerging Euro-democracy involves not just individuals and classes of individuals but well-entrenched historical collectivities (i.e., states) that themselves are significantly different in terms of their size, development, competitiveness, consumption levels, and so forth, and hence are even more sensitive to political disparities and policy distributions at the point of institutional departure than would be individuals or social classes within a given preexistent society.
2. The popular expectations of individuals about improvements at the Euro-polity level are much more vague and "projective" than are the corresponding expectations at the national level. Until and unless the former become more firmly fixed in the calculations of individuals (and organized into European scale units of action), it seems unlikely that entrenched national politicians can be outbid for support.
3. Since the Treaty of European Union enshrined it, these very same politicians can often plausibly invoke the principle of subsidiarity to protect the local or national status quo from "unwarranted" intrusions by a prospective Euro-democracy that would equalize rights and regulations for the Euro-polity as a whole—and, thereby, override national peculiarities in the name of a more general public interest.

In the absence of some manifest collapse of the *anciens régimes nationaux*, as sometimes occurred within the autocracies of Southern Europe and Latin America and even more dramatically in Eastern Europe, it is not clear whether these two generic dilemmas can be sufficiently overcome to allow for any substantial progress toward Euro-democratization. Perhaps the gradual accumulation of firmer popular expectations of equality, security, and recognition at that level will suffice, but it is more likely that an intervening crisis of legitimacy in existing EU institutions will preempt that slow and uneven process. Mere malperformance and declining policy competence in the member states are not likely to be sufficient to compel actors to shift their allegiances.

The two Euro-specific dilemmas are no less daunting. Both have to do with the unprecedented nature of the enterprise. First, if, as I have presumed, the nonstate Euro-polity will have to come up with novel institutions in order to democratize itself, then both politicians and citizens may have considerable difficulty in recognizing these novel rules and practices as "democratic." While there is already a considerable range of variance within member states in what they consider democratic, the shift to a much larger scale and, in all probability, diminished scope of public authority is bound to mean experimenting with forms of representation, citizenship, and accountability of rulers that do not yet exist and whose consequences are rather unpredictable. The more novel (and, perhaps, functionally appropriate) these citizen rights and decision rules are, the greater the initial obstacles to their being accorded legitimacy. On the other hand, following the "time-tested" ways of a federal or confederal nature will only be ineffectual or counterproductive—if my nonstate hypothesis holds. Admittedly, Publius in the *Federalist Papers* was fully aware of this dilemma and did a masterful job of overcoming it, but will the more diverse, distracted, and, perhaps, skeptical publics of contemporary Europe prove so easy to persuade?

Second, filling the Euro-polity's democracy deficit with novel rights and rules will not only have to satisfy the already diverse set of actual member states, but it will also have to be sufficiently flexible, open, and "acceptable" to incorporate an indeterminate number of future members over an, as yet, undefined territory.

Moreover, the eastern, southeastern, and southern (Mediterranean) countries in which this expansion will have to take place have even greater levels of diversity in development and culture and are much less settled in terms of their domestic regime characteristics. Those founders of the United States faced a roughly analogous situation in that they certainly envisaged that their constitution would be applied to a westward expanding population and set of new units, but it is doubtful that they envisaged anything like the economic, social, cultural, and political diversity that the Euro-polity will have to absorb.[18]

HOW SHOULD A EURO-DEMOCRACY BE CONFIGURED?

My first assumption is that—because, in the immediate future, the Euro-polity is likely to retain the status of a "nonstate and nonnation"—it would be inappropriate and even counterproductive to define its citizens, representatives, and rulers in the usual manner for a large-scale, socially heterogenous, advanced capitalist nation-state, that is, in the manner of a federal polity.

The core of the emerging Euro-polity's novelty lies in *the growing dissociation between territorial constituencies and functional competences.* In the classic model of the state (if not invariably in the praxis of specific states), the exercise of public authority in different functional domains is coincident or congruent with a specific and unique territory.[19] When one arrives at its physical borders, the legitimate exercise of coercion in all these domains ends. The polity on the other side has, in principle, no right to command obedience in any domain on one's own side—and there presumably exists no superordinate entity exercising authority over both sides.

Not even the initial contours of such an institutional coincidence can be detected in the Euro-polity as presently constituted. Instead, the distribution of territorial and functional powers has remained indeterminate and inconsistent in decisive respects. Even a cursory examination of the territorial organization of the EU makes clear that the boundary between insiders and outsiders remains uncertain and/or follows no uniform criterion. This is especially the case with monetary unification, a core area of the TEU. For instance, it was foreseen that those member states that did not fulfill the convergence criteria would be suspended from participation in Stage III of Economic and Monetary Union (Article 109j). Moreover, Great Britain, Denmark, and Sweden have reserved the right to decide whether they will eventually participate in it.

Great Britain also remained explicitly exempt (until 1998) from the commitment to a common social policy. Article 198a empowers local and regional subunits to participate in an advisory Committee of Regions. While the relevant clauses fix the number of committee members for the individual member states, they leave the conception of local and regional units unspecified. Nor is there a clear and uniformly binding distribution of functional *compétences* among the territorial units of the EU. Whereas the treaty declares that "decisions are taken as closely as possible to the citizen" (Article A) and that the goals of the union are to be realized "respecting the principle of subsidiarity" (Article B), the concrete implications of this principle are left to subsequent intergovernmental agreements (and eventual judgments of the European Court of Justice).

The functional distribution of *compétences* has also become even more diffuse through the creation of new European organizations and coordinating mechanisms. This is, for instance, apparent in the establishment of a joint conference of the national parliaments and the European Parliament that can form and meet "as necessary" (Declaration on the Conference of the Parliaments); in the exceedingly complex codecision procedure of the European Parliament, the council, and the commission on a broad range of issues (Articles 189b, 189c); and in the proto-corporatist procedures outlined for the area of social policy, according to which the commission can call on the "Social Partners" to draft relevant measures, which could even preempt European Community action and lead to independent private contracts implemented either through the member states or through the European Union itself (Agreement on Social Policy, Articles 3 and 4). On questions of foreign and security policy, a political committee was created as a sort of embryonic foreign office, but with *compétences* in relation to the other organs of the EU that are only vaguely delineated. In defense policy, the WEU is named as an "integral part of the development of the European Union" (Article J4), but its relationship to existing EC bodies is left indeterminate. Moreover, the TEU makes it clear that there will be no necessary coincidence between membership in the EU and in the WEU. The latter will be open to all present and future members of the EU, but there is no obligation to join.

So, in the emergent Euro-polity, the functional and the territorial domains of authority have become less rather than more congruent over time. What seems to be asserting, and even consolidating, itself is a plurality of polities at different levels of aggregation—national, subnational, and supranational—that overlap in a multitude of domains. Moreover, the EU authorities have few exclusive *compétences* and have yet to assert their hierarchical control over member states—except via the limited jurisprudence of the European Court of Justice and in such restricted functional domains as competition policy. Instead, these multiple levels negotiate with each other in a continuous way in order to perform common tasks and resolve common problems across an expanding range of issues. Without sovereignty—without a definitive and superordinate center for the resolution of conflicts or for the allocation of public goods—there is only a process and hence no definite person or body that can be held accountable for its actions in the public realm. Moreover, the participants in this process are not just a fixed number of national states but an enormous variety of subnational units and networks, supranational associations, and transnational firms.

To make the point clearer, I ask the reader to try to imagine a polity that did *not* have the following:

1. a locus of clearly defined, unchallengeable supreme authority;
2. an established, central hierarchy of public offices;

3. a predefined and distinctive sphere of competence within which it can make decisions binding on all;
4. a fixed and contiguous territory over which it exercised authority;
5. an exclusive recognition by other polities, membership in international organizations, and capacity to conclude international treaties;
6. an overarching identity and symbolic presence for its subjects/citizens;
7. an established and effective monopoly over the legitimate means of coercion;
8. a unique capacity for the direct implementation of its decisions upon intended individuals and groups; and
9. an exclusive capacity for controlling the movement of goods, services, capital, and persons within its borders.

However, say such a polity *did* have the capability to make decisions, resolve conflicts, produce public goods, coordinate private behavior, regulate markets, hold elections, respond to interest pressures, generate revenue, allocate expenditures, and even declare and wage war! If you can do this, you will have succeeded in at least mentally superseding the limits imposed by the nation-state on our habitual ways of thinking about politics, although it may still be difficult for you to imagine how such a "postsovereign, pretero-national, multilayered, overlapping, indefinite" arrangement of authority could possibly be stable in the longer run.

Elsewhere, I have argued that the EU is likely to become something qualitatively different, neither an intergovernmental *confederatio* nor a supranational *stato/federatio* but one of two novel forms of political domination I have called a *consortio* or a *condominio*.[20]

As an ideal type, the *consortio* assumes a fixed and irreversible set of member states within defined territorial boundaries, but with varying policy responsibilities (the expression "*L'Europe à géometrie variable*" seems to capture this property well). Subsets of members would pool their capacity to act autonomously in domains that they could no longer govern at their own level of aggregation but would be free to determine—either at the moment of joining or when subsequent revisions were made—which specific common obligations they were willing to accept. Presumably, they would form a singular and relatively contiguous spatial bloc, but they would arrange their common affairs within a multitude of distinctive functional authorities, only some of which would be coordinated from a single center or even served by a common secretariat.

The emergence of something resembling an ideal-type *condominio* would be an even more unprecedented outcome—that is, the one that least resembles the preexisting Euro-state system. In it, both territorial as well as functional constituencies would vary. Not only would each member country be able to select from a menu of potential common tasks, but each

European institution would be composed of a different (although presumably overlapping) set of members. Instead of a single Europe with recognized and contiguous boundaries, there would be many Europes: a trading Europe, an energy Europe, an environmental Europe, a social welfare Europe, even a defense Europe, and so forth. Instead of one "Eurocracy" that coordinated all the distinct tasks involved in the integration process, there would be multiple regional institutions acting autonomously to solve common problems and produce different public goods. Given its formidable coordination problems—not to mention its unprecedented nature—one can hardly imagine the deliberate establishment of such a cumbersome arrangement. It could only emerge in an improvised and incremental fashion from successive compromises among members with divergent interests and institutional legacies.

If either of these models better describes the medium-term outcome than those that lie on the more orthodox continuum connecting the intergovernmental organization with the supranational state—something that admittedly is a matter of conjecture—and if democratization cannot be indefinitely postponed, then it seems reasonable to me to presume that the Euro-polity will have to invent and implement new forms of ruler accountability, new rights and obligations for citizens, and new channels for territorial and functional representation. For all existing conceptions of democracy—with the limited exception of those involving small-scale, highly localized forms of direct democracy—presume the existence of a political unit with the minimal properties of a state. Only if there is a ruling person or body with a legitimate command of legitimate violence can it be made accountable to citizens through the appropriate channels of representation. Without such a prior coincidence between external and internal sovereignty, the most that one can expect is a *confederatio* or intergovernmental arrangement that does not itself have to be democratic.

My assumption is that the process of European integration has irrevocably crossed the threshold of intergovernmentalism, but it is still far removed from reaching that "indispensable" coincidence of territorial and functional authority that is the foundation of stateness—not to mention the even more elusive property of a common identity that is the foundation of *nationhood*.

The main strategic implication I have drawn from this is that the democratization of the EU can be postponed, but not indefinitely. At the present moment, there is no grassroots movement clamoring for greater participation and access in order to make its rulers more accountable—just a diffuse (but growing) public dissatisfaction with its remote and opaque modus operandi. Nevertheless, the EU has made itself sufficiently omniscient, controversial, and indispensable in the lives of Europeans that its "real-existing" practices cannot simply be tolerated or ignored.

To those who, recognizing the dilemma, claim that the answer lies in revising and reinforcing the capacity of national democracies to control what is going on within the EU, I would reply that not only is this likely to be insufficient, given the lack of decisional autonomy at that level, but such a shift in strategy and expectations might also deprive the integration process of its dynamic ability to resolve conflicts and generate the sort of public goods to which Europeans have become increasingly accustomed.

To those who, welcoming the prospect of the EU's losing its integrative dynamic, argue that it is high time to reign in this increasingly obtrusive organization, I would respond that it is not clear whether this can be accomplished without endangering what has already been accomplished—that famous *acquis communautaire*. And that *acquis* consists not just of the four freedoms for the movement of goods, services, capital, and persons with all the private benefits that accrue to them, but it may also include an even more important acquisition—namely, the transformation of the European state system into what Karl Deutsch and others have called a "pluralistic security community" within which all participants are confident that their conflicts will never be resolved by the use of force, or even the threat of it.[21]

Proponents of integration like to rely on the analogy of a bicycle to describe it: unless it continues to move forward or even if the process begins to lose momentum, it risks toppling over and throwing its riders back where they came from. Its opponents presumably believe that the analogy should be that of a tricycle that can be parked safely whenever and wherever one wishes. Frankly, there is no way that we can know which is the proper analogy for the EU in its present condition,[22] but even the remotest prospect that the Europe conveyance might tip over (and, after all, even tricycles do this occasionally) should be regarded with alarm. Reverting to its *statu quo ante integratio* of pervasive anarchy, constant threats of violence and unstable balances of power punctuated by international war would most certainly be against the interests of almost everyone.

So, if I am also correct in assuming that the strategy that has guided integration since its origins in the European Coal and Steel Community (i.e., the famous Monnet Method with its reliance on functional interdependence, indirection, unintended consequences, spillovers from one issue area to another, and package deals that increase the scope and level of common institutions) is no longer capable of providing further momentum to the process—pace the impending prospect of monetary unification—then a more overtly political strategy based on democratization might be able to take up the slack. However, if and when this happens, its promoters are going to have to invent novel forms of citizenship, channels of representation, and rules for decision making that are specifically appropriate for the emerging Euro-polity.

NOTES

1. I have substantiated this in "Examining the Present Euro-Polity with the Help of Past Theories" in *Governance in the European Union,* ed. Gary Marks, Fritz Scharpf, Philippe C. Schmitter, and Wolfgang Streeck (London: Sage, 1996), 1–14.

2. The literature on the so-called "democracy deficit" of the EU is enormous and, by and large, substantiates the observation that its existing institutional configuration falls considerably short of being democratic. As one wag put it, "Since the EC requires that its member be democratic, if the EC were ever to apply to join itself, it would have to turn itself down." What is also (if less overtly) presumed is that there is no "indirect" or "functionalist" strategy that can fill this deficit. Hence, its members will have to agree "formally and intergovernmentally"—if and when it becomes imperative to address the issue.

3. Elsewhere, I have explored the four factors that seem (to me) to be pushing the EU in such contrary directions: (a) the problem of enlargement—especially to the east, (b) the increase in the politicization of integration issues, (c) the growing implementation deficit, and (d) the rising need to deal with issues of European security after the Cold War.

Note the tacit implication that the democratization deficit alone has (so far and for the foreseeable future) *not* been of sufficient magnitude to compel the member states to make a serious good-faith effort to eliminate it, even though some of the impetus behind the rising controversiality and wider public attention to EU affairs (politicization) probably has something to do with a general increase in questioning the democratic legitimacy of EU procedures and policies. See "The Future Euro-Polity and Its Impact upon Private Interest Governance within Member States," *Droit et société* 28 (1994): 659–76.

4. The issue of how to label this emerging nonstate order poses a series of difficulties. I have rejected *confederal* or *quasi-federal* because these terms would limit the possible options to the existing continuum that runs between an intergovernmental organization and a supranational state when it is precisely my contention that the Euro-polity is more likely to evolve toward (and, to a certain extent, already is) something quite different.

Elsewhere, I have proposed neo-Latin terms, *consortio* and *condominio*, to capture two of the alternatives in which either the functional or the territorial and the functional components of political order would vary from one member to another over an extended period of time. "Imagining the Future of the Euro-Polity with the Help of New Concepts," in *Governance in the European Union,* ed. Marks et al., 21–50.

I might have used *Euro-OPNI* ("European *objet politique nonidentifié*") in honor of Jacques Delors, who once used this expression to (sort of) define what the EC/EU was and would remain for the foreseeable future, but I decided to forego that opportunity. *Eurarchy* was another alternative, *eurocracy* having already been taken to describe the commission bureaucracy in Brussels. Unfortunately, the two are so close that using the former would inevitably occasion some (pernicious) confusion with the latter. Thus, I have decided in this book to stick with the innocuous label *Euro-polity.*

5. For my first effort at addressing this issue, see my "Alternatives for the Future European Polity: Is Federalism the Only Answer?" in *Démocratie et construction européenne,* ed. Mario Telò (Brussels: Editions de l'Université de Bruxelles, 1995), 349–61.

6. It should be observed that, if the EU had not already expanded beyond the limits of intergovernmental cooperation, the issue of its democratization would be moot. There is no compelling reason that citizens would expect such an arrangement to be accountable—provided that their own democratically accountable rulers could either veto its actions or withdraw from its jurisdiction with little or no effort.

7. See Philippe C. Schmitter and Terry Karl. "What Democracy Is ... and Is Not," *Journal of Democracy* 2, no. 3 (Summer 1991): 75–88.

8. For better or worse, the future of Euro-democracy rests with the set of institutions called—following the Treaty of Maastricht (1992)—the European Union (EU). Formerly, it was given the name of the European Economic Community (EEC) and, then, the European Community (EC) when the secretariats of the European Coal and Steel Community, Euratom, and the EEC were merged in 1972. There are many other, independent European-level institutions, not the least of which is the Council of Europe, which contribute to the orderly and, sometimes, democratic governance of this part of the world, but no one seems to doubt that the EEC/EC/EU is destined to be preeminent among them.

9. In fact, it is at least arguable that, since the TEU in its Article 138a specifically mentions the role that European political parties should play in the integration process, this particular channel of representation gets more of a formal recognition at the European level than in the constitutions of most, if not all, of its member states.

10. See Jane Mansbridge, *Beyond Adversarial Democracy* (New York: Basic Books, 1980).

11. It would be more accurate to say that "accountability appears to be ensured in a way that satisfies the legitimate expectations of the citizenry," since this can vary rather considerably from one political culture to another. Needless to say, in the context of contemporary Europe, national differences over such things as "parliamentary sovereignty," "party government," "transparency in the actions of public officials," and so forth, will make it all the more difficult to arrive at a consensual perception of what is involved in accountability.

12. Hence, it is very unlikely to emerge from the interpretative procedures that the European Court of Justice has resorted to in order to convert the Treaty of Rome into a quasi-constitution. Indeed, it is resistance to the further expansion of these norms that may provide one of the strongest incentives for explicit constitutionalization.

13. I am much indebted in the following section to Dario Castiglione, "Contracts and Constitutions," *in Democracy and Constitutional Culture in the Union of Europe,* ed. R. Bellamy, V. Bufacchi, and D. Castiglione (London: Lothian Foundation Press, 1995): 59–79.

14. *Pace* Ken Jowitt who has argued that the European Community is already a "charismatic project" and only likely to advance further under the inspiration of more charisma: "No More Normans in Europe," a talk given to the

Seminar/Forum on Sovereignty and Governance, Institute of International Studies, Stanford University, January 19, 1996. Nothing in my view is less likely to lead to the refounding or revising of EU institutions. Even if a charismatic leader or movement should emerge, and even if he or she would attempt to create more democratic institutions at the level of Europe, my supposition is that the effort would be as dismal a failure as all the preceding efforts by national charismatics at consolidating democracy—from Sekou Touré, Kwame Nukrumah, and Nassar to Alain Garcia, Fernando Collor, and Alberto Fujimori. For the original version of this notion, see—not Max Weber—David Apter, *Ghana in Transition* (New York: Atheneum, 1963).

15. Nor are they likely to be able to "take over" a parliamentary mandate to introduce minor reforms and then draft an entirely new document as did the U.S. founding fathers in what could only be called a *coup constitutionnel.* In contemporary Europe, the member states and their respective citizenries are much too attentive to permit such a distortion of mandate.

16. And, hence, these dilemmas have been discussed in greater detail in my forthcoming *Essaying the Consolidation of Democracy,* which deals exclusively with the processes of recent democratization at the national level in Southern Europe, Latin America, and Eastern Europe.

17. *After the Revolution: Authority in a Good Society* (New Haven, Conn.: Yale University Press, 1970).

18. The one issue of diversity that these American founding fathers tried to finesse—slavery—proved to be irresolvable within the framework of their constitution. I doubt if the founders of Euro-democracy would be willing even to contemplate anything as horrendous as the U.S. Civil War as a way of eventually resolving those issues of diversity that could not be dealt with initially.

19. And, in the nation-state model, these domains are supposed to be coterminous with a distinctive and unique national identity based on a common language, culture, descent group, or "community of fate" (*Schicksalsgemeinschaft*).

20. I have subsequently discovered that I am not alone in concluding that the EU may be heading for novelty. Ben Rosamund, for example, has suggested that "integration may be coaxing (or perhaps even is) the evolution of new state forms which are not nation-states." "Mapping the European Condition: Theory of Integration and the Integration of Theory," *European Journal of International Relations* 1, no. 3 (September 1995): 403.

My presumption is that the EU is not becoming either a nation or a state. In addition to my "Imagining the Future of the Euro-Polity with the Help of New Concepts," cited in n. 4, see my "If the Nation-State Were to Wither Away in Europe, What Might Replace It?" in *The Future of the Nation State,* ed. Svante Gustavsson and Leif Lewin (Stockholm: Nerenius & Santeris and Routledge, 1996), 211–44.

21. *Political Community and the North Atlantic Area* (Princeton, N.J.: Princeton University Press, 1957).

22. The often remarked-on institutional stagnation of the mid-1960s to the mid-1970s was only a relative matter that disguised a good deal of forward, if less visible, momentum (especially in the field of European jurisprudence), so that it does not constitute a fair test between the competing analogies.

2

Citizenship

Citizenship has become a much discussed, if still unresolved, concept. It seems to begin with the acquisition of a *status* or *condition,* protected by law, that grants to a select group—usually native-born (*jus solis*) or genetically correct (*jus sanguinis*) adults—a general equality of opportunity and treatment with respect to a (varied) bundle of rights and obligations. It becomes a *practice* or *process* whereby those who have that status make use of it—politically, legally, administratively, economically, and socially—to reduce their uncertainties and satisfy their interests. Presumably, it terminates in a *result* or *product* that is legitimacy (i.e., the integration of citizens in conformity to the norms and practices of the polity that granted them the status in the first place).

Needless to say, in the real world, there are lots of potential disjunctures in this scenario. The distribution of the status may be too narrow or the content of the rights too restricted to protect citizens from arbitrary treatment, social discrimination, or economic exploitation. The beneficiaries of the process may exploit their favored status to increase the uncertainty of others and/or to satisfy their interests at the expense of the resident aliens ("denizens") who are excluded. The outcome of the process may not always be to generate a single sense of loyalty or community but might even convince some citizens that another regime or polity could offer them greater security or satisfaction. For it is important to stress that the granting of citizenship logically involves a complex set of choices about inclusion and exclusion and was closely linked historically to the development of national consciousness and the emergence of the nation-state as the dominant form of political organization in Europe.

In a justly famous essay, T. H. Marshall suggested that the content of citizenship has evolved over time. As he reconstructed the process for

23

Great Britain, initial concessions by authorities provided a lever that could be wielded to demand others, and these, in turn, led to further claims for equal treatment. It began in the eighteenth century with the struggle for equal rights and obligations before the law, expanded in the nineteenth century to cover equal formal participation in political life, especially through universal suffrage, and in the twentieth century shifted its attention to equal opportunity to share in the country's material and cultural heritage, especially through state provision of welfare.[1] Marshall's sequential account is logically satisfying, but it is certainly not historically generalizable or functionally imperative. Both France and Germany took rather different routes to reach, more or less, the same bundle of rights and obligations in the end.

It is also not clear from Marshall's analysis whether the process of citizenship has terminated with the attainment of the contemporary welfare state or whether that merely places new levers in the hands of more actors demanding further extensions of equal rights (and, to a lesser extent, equal obligations). Ralf Dahrendorf, for one, sees a serious danger in pushing its principles into new domains:

> The extension of citizenship has reached in recent years, the apparently insurmountable walls of ascribed status. Men and women are not merely to be given the suffrage and equal wages for equal work, but they are supposed to be treated as equals in all respects; society is to be arranged in such a way that the differences can be ignored.[2]

From his account, it is not clear whether he regards such an eventuality as a social impossibility or rejects it because of the state intervention it would require.

But what if the next Marshallian extension did not involve empowering those who are already national citizens with new rights and obligations in existing polities but transposing some of those that they already have and creating some new ones at a different, more encompassing level of aggregation? That is, what if the next stage involved the status/condition, process/practice, and eventual result/product of *European* citizenship?

FACING THE "SPECTER" OF EURO-CITIZENSHIP

The Treaty of European Union already does this formally in its Articles 8, 8a, 8b, 8c, 8d, and 8e, which outline an initial set of rights.[3] The last of these even invites the Council of Ministers "acting unanimously" and only on a proposal from the commission and only after consultation with the European Parliament to strengthen or to add to this list in the future.

But what could the EU do to further empower its citizens that is not already better and more securely provided by its respective member states? To do this, we first have to look a bit more closely at the concept of citizenship itself.

Roger Brubaker has recently laid out for us the six "membership norms" that he claims define the ideal-typical conception of citizenship.[4] According to this model, membership should be:

1. *Unitary*—all holders of the status should have full rights and obligations.
2. *Sacred*—citizens must be willing to make sacrifices for the state or community that grants them the status.
3. *National*—membership must be based on a community that is simultaneously political and cultural.
4. *Democratic*—citizens should be entitled to participate significantly in the business of rule, and access to citizenship should be open to all residents so that, in the long run, residence in the community and citizenship in it will coincide.
5. *Unique*—each citizen should belong to one and only one political community.
6. *Consequential*—citizenship must entail important social and political privileges that distinguish its holders from noncitizens.

These six normative criteria could be applied, *mutatis mutandis*, to any efforts at "citizenizing" the Euro-polity. Even so, the potential reformer should tread cautiously since, as Brubaker himself notes:

> this model of citizenship is largely vestigial. That it survives is due less to its own normative force than to the lack of a coherent and persuasive alternative. It is, moreover, significantly out of phase with the contemporary realities of state-membership.[5]

Moreover, I propose to add a seventh criterion that I presume to have been implicit in Brubaker's list but that deserves to be discussed (and questioned) explicitly:

7. *Individual*—citizenship is an attribute that can only be possessed and exercised by individual human beings, although adult parents may be considered to be acting in lieu of their children and hence for the family as a collective unit.

With these seven criteria and Brubaker's warning in mind, let us then evaluate what might be involved in developing European citizenship.

UNITARY

Here, the ideal normative imperative is that the status of "citizen of the European Union" should be general, as well as equal. In principle, no adult person (or, as we shall see, no recognized organization) should be subject to only some of its rights and obligations, and none should enjoy special treatment. In practice, this would mean retaining, in the strictest sense, the *acquis communautaire* such that all member states and all citizens of those states would have identical rights and obligations.

Now this is precisely what is *not* likely to happen if either a *consortial* or a *condominial* fate awaits the EU. In both cases (with different degrees of freedom), members will be enabled to choose from different packages of rights and obligations—and the impact of this will extend *a fortiori* to their citizens. For example, freedom of movement and establishment could vary over time and perhaps across professions or issue arenas; the right of individuals or firms to transfer funds or to open anonymous bank accounts may not be the same for everyone; some member states might even grant all citizens of other EU countries resident in their territories full voting rights, and others might restrict it to the present objective of voting only in local elections; a self-selected "social democratic" subset of countries could move toward full equivalence in their social security and health insurance systems—even establishing common pension funds and budgetary arrangements—while another "neoliberal" subset could even be dismantling their social safety nets and privatizing their health care systems—and so forth. All would depend on the pattern of future treaty adhesions, as it does now for Euro-citizens depending on whether their respective states have signed such documents as the Schengen Agreement or demanded *dérogations* from such specific obligations as the Monetary Union or the Social Charter.

SACRED

This principle has already been considerably attenuated for individuals at the national level. Not only has citizenship been somewhat "secularized," at least in the western part of Europe, by the decline in militant nationalism and rigidly ethnic definitions of collective identity, but the "heavy" and "mystical" obligations historically linked to it have also declined. With the abolition of military conscription and militia-type armies in several countries, individuals are no longer required to die for their nation or state.[6] The various symbolic allegiances expected of citizens (e.g., flag saluting and anthem singing) have become increasingly ritualistic,[7] and one hears less that classic slogan of unreflective national allegiance: "My country, right or wrong!"

All this bodes well for an even less sacred (and hence more attenuated) conception of Euro-citizenship. Individuals and organizations would have a common obligation to obey the law, especially the supremacy of EU law as interpreted by the European Court of Justice (ECJ). They would agree to transfer a (small) proportion of their taxes to EU institutions, although their net contributions might differ considerably depending on the bundle of functions chosen or the effect of *juste retour*. They should be willing to help others in time of emergency, treat fellow Europeans with respect and tolerance in their increasingly frequent exchanges, and be prepared to re-distribute some benefits or make concessions in the name of solidarity and the eventual social cohesion of Europe as a whole. That last item is, of course, the most difficult because the territorial and functional parameters of that unit are not yet known, and the internal variation within these pa-rameters in terms of development levels, language use, cultural norms, and political tendencies is considerably greater than the variation con-tained within any of its member states.

What is still far from clear is the role that the EU (or any "affiliated" re-gional organization) will eventually play with regard to collective security and defense policy. Historically, the obligation to serve in the defense of one's country and the common experiences that have ensued from this (at least, for males) have been extremely important in the development of a sense of common fate and shared sacrifice, which, in turn, contributed to cementing the tie between state membership and national identity. Should the EU move in this direction, not only would it have to acquire far more "statelike" properties than it currently has in order to coordinate and fi-nance such a collective effort, but also it would be very likely to generate a more sacred (and perhaps controversial) relationship with "its" citizens. This would be the case even if, as has been happening in the member states, recruitment to the armed forces involved would be purely volun-tary, selective, and professional. There is nothing like the experience—di-rect or vicarious—of combating a common enemy to feed the flames of sacredness.[8]

NATIONAL

Nowhere have the strict principles of citizenship diminished more than on this item. It is no longer so preposterous to describe oneself as "a citizen of the world" or, at least, of something beyond the nation-state. Admit-tedly, the *Eurobaromètre* data on public opinion do not show any monot-onic tendency toward an increasing sense of "feeling European" or of being "a citizen of Europe"—indeed, this personal identification has de-creased rather than increased in the aftermath of the Single European Act and the Treaty of European Union.[9] Nevertheless, the sentiment is much more prevalent among younger people and could pick up and even accumulate across generations in the future.

More to the point, the act of acquiring citizenship used to imply the joining of a coherent, well-defined national community with its own homogeneous culture—and, of course, of only being allowed to join one such community. In many countries, this involved a lengthy and demanding "apprenticeship" in national laws and mores.[10] First, foreigners were made into natives and then—and only then—were they granted citizen status. Indeed, naturalized second-generation immigrants were often said to behave "more like Americans than the Americans." Nowadays, those becoming citizens can insist that they be allowed to retain their culture of origin and not be thrown into the "melting pot." They may even legitimately demand that the state of which they have become a citizen should subsidize and protect their subcultures from discrimination and attenuation. In short, citizenship for individuals is no longer an assurance of membership in a correspondingly unique national culture.[11]

But how far can this go? Is it possible to draw enough personal satisfaction out of belonging to a "community" that does not have a common *ethnie*, language, religion, mores, or lifestyle? Would this not be so attenuated a sense of membership that appeals for sacrifice or solidarity would fail to invoke any response—much less one that would allow the "supranation" to respond as a unit to an external crisis or redistribute benefits consensually within its internal borders?[12]

Inversely, why should individuals (and, for that matter, organizations) in the Euro-polity have to be "nationals" in some sense in order to act like citizens? Why could they not be loyal to a common set of institutions and political/legal principles rather than to some mystical charismatic founder or set of mythologized ancestors? Why could Renan's *plébiscite de tous les jours* not be about rights and procedures in the present, rather than sacrifices and glories of the past?[13]

That, it seems to me, is the major issue. Not whether the eventual Euro-polity will be able to reproduce on an enlarged scale the same intensity of collective sentiment that was once characteristic of its member nation-states, but whether it can produce an encompassing system of stable and peaceful political relations without such a passionately shared identity or community of fate. Admittedly, this places a heavy burden on interest calculation and instrumental reason at a time when it is more fashionable to presume the rising importance of collective enthusiasms and consumatory values. And admittedly, there are several cases out there of plurinational polities that have recently broken up or are currently being threatened with secession, seemingly in defiance of national interest and confirmation of passionate belief. If, as some believe, the postindustrial, postmodern condition necessarily entails precisely such a shift from the rational to the emotional, then the very notion of citizenship in a nonnation would be oxymoronic. If, as I am inclined to believe, this condition is not so constraining, then, nonnational citizenship may not be such a far-fetched possibility. Indeed, it may become a commonplace in the future.

DEMOCRATIC

This is the most crucial principle from the perspective of this essay. For the EU to succeed in regaining its momentum and reestablishing its legitimacy, its member-states will have to agree on reforms that not only make its institutions function more effectively but also make its rulers more accountable to its citizenry. In the traditional conception of citizenship, the way of doing this is to increase the *political participation* of adult individuals—by granting them the right to vote in contested elections, to present themselves as candidates for representative positions, to form and join associations, to speak out publicly and petition authorities for redress, to consult and be consulted on matters of policy, and even—in direct democracies—to be physically present and decide on all issues binding on the community. A secondary concern is *openness* or *transparency* (i.e., rendering the conditions under which binding public choices are made accessible to more actors and, most particularly, to those who had been previously excluded or discriminated against).

This is not the place for a disquisition on the increased impoverishment of individual participation in the democracies of EU member states. In almost all of them, voter abstention has increased. Trade unions have lost members. Traditional parties have lost militants and core voters. Individuals identify less and less with a particular party. And the reputation of politicians is at an all-time low. Nor is there space for a discussion of the increased opaqueness of national public policy making under the influence of the sheer complexity of the problems they are required to deal with and the consequent role that technocratic expertise plays in their resolution.

The German term *Öffentlichkeit*, as developed by Jürgen Habermas, captures a good deal of the dilemma.[14] Under ideal conditions, democracies should arrive at their decisions through a process of disclosure and deliberation in which citizens—collective as well as individual—restrict their actions and positions to those that are publicly visible and defensible. In actual practice, organized subgroups of citizens use their privileged resources to hire specialists to represent their particular interests, and these professional representatives, in turn, collude with rulers to arrive in less than public ways at arrangements that are subsequently proclaimed to be "in the public interest."

(It should be noted that some theories of democratic citizenship would go a good deal further than merely ensuring the opportunity for participation and openness. These would insist that individuals [and the organizations they form] be themselves "internally democratic." The former should be respectful of authority, other regarding, tolerant, and willing to compromise; that is, individuals should have a "civic culture." Their parties, associations, and movements should not only be all of the above but also conduct competitive elections for their leaders, guarantee the rights of minority factions in their midst, and faithfully keep their commitments with members and authorities! Needless to say, national polities have, by and large, given up on insisting on internal democracy. The capacity for indoctrinating their citizens with a singular conception of civic values and for monitoring the internal politics of their representative organizations is simply too limited—and the effort to do either would conflict with other democratic rights and practices.)

What forms of participation and *Öffentlichkeit* can the EU possibly offer its citizens that would not compete with or displace those that already exist in the member states? Recognizing that national citizens have been reducing their levels of participation and that most national polities have become more secretive and less transparent, is it at all likely that the emerging Euro-polity could do anything to reverse such antidemocratic trends?

Of course, the EU has already attempted to do some things for individuals. Direct elections for the European Parliament since 1979 were supposed to produce more participation—and have had very little effect other than revealing that citizens are much more preoccupied with exploiting them to send "messages of disgruntlement" to their national politicians.[15] Moreover, these elections are even losing their appeal for this purpose; voter abstention in them has grown monotonically in almost all member countries.[16] The TEU broke new ground by enfranchising residents of other EU member states to vote and run as candidates in local elections—which could be the first step in extending the right to all Euro-citizens to vote in all elections in the constituencies where they permanently reside, regardless of their national citizenship.

This very same treaty reaffirmed the rights of individuals to petition the European Parliament and created an ombudsman's office at the EU level.[17] This person has finally been chosen after a lengthy squabble; it remains to be seen whether he will be successful in opening up a new conduit for individual access. This same treaty also pledged to make the proceedings of various EU institutions more "transparent." If initial reaction to a timid effort during the Danish presidency to publicize the discussions and voting behavior in the Council of Ministers is any portent, it seems doubtful that much will be accomplished at this level in the future.[18] On the contrary, the commission has made greater progress along these lines, although some of its initial public relations efforts have been widely ridiculed.[19]

Of course, since its very foundation the Euro-polity has distinctively privileged the participation of functional interest associations—especially those organized by business interests at a European level—in its deliberations. It has even encouraged the formation and subsidized the activities of many such organizations—without, however, much success in instauring the stable Euro-corporatist arrangements they desired.[20] The informal system of representation that has emerged is much more pluralist (multiple, nonhierarchic, overlapping, and voluntaristic) in nature and manifestly skewed to favor the interests of business. The formal Economic and Social Council with its officially nominated members representing business, labor, and "other" interests has proven to be utterly ineffectual since its founding in the Treaty of Rome.

More recently, both the commission and the parliament have gotten around to registering and regulating the associations and movements that lobby them, although they insist that, in so doing, they have no intention of creating a privileged—much less a monopolistic—set of organizational citizens or of imposing strict criteria of representativeness upon them. The register will be open to all and access will be, at least formally, equal. No effort will even be made to favor those that are distinctively European in scope, as opposed to those that represent local, provincial, or national interests and passions.[21] This brings up the issue of participation by and openness to yet another set of democratic constituencies: the territorial subunits of national member polities. By its very nature as the product of an international treaty, the EU was created exclusively by existing sovereign states. Their *Länder*, *regioni*, *provinces*, *estados autonómicos*, municipalities, and so forth, enjoyed no special status. If they were interested in participating, the only channel that seemed to be open to them was to pass through their respective national governments. Nevertheless (and, in some cases, despite considerable resistance by these governments), these subnational regions and cities gradually established their own structures of representation—to the extent that almost fifty of them have quasi-embassies in Brussels.[22] Again, the TEU took a modest step in a more democratic direction when it created a consultative *Comité des Régions*, leaving it, however, to the national governments to establish the criteria for which units would be represented and how they would be chosen.

All this does indicate some effort to address the twin issues of participation and openness, even if the channels that have been created so far either lead to relatively powerless institutions or remain highly skewed in terms of the citizens that have effective access to them. Certainly, none seems to have seized the imagination of the public or to have dramatically changed the accountability of EU authorities. Future increases in the po-

litical role of the European Parliament and possible changes in the system
for electing MEPs might improve the situation but are unlikely to transform it substantially.

UNIQUE

This is a quality that presently seems almost anachronistic at the individual level and would definitely have to be abrogated in the development of
Euro-citizenship for both individuals and organizations. Many persons
now have dual national citizenships without this causing great confusion
or corruption. Even resident foreigners (denizens) who formerly were denied the right to organize and petition—often on the alleged grounds that
this would interfere in the internal affairs of their country of origin—now
have virtually the same political rights as national citizens. Once the tight
link between citizenship and national culture had been loosened, this sort
of an evolution became an obvious adjustment to an increasingly interde-
pendent and physically mobile world. Individual firms and persons, regardless of their formal national status, have been allowed (de facto if not
de jure) to join and contribute to as many national and international associations or movements as they wish, in as many countries as they live or
operate. And these associations or movements are allowed to operate in
more than one political jurisdiction—beneath or beyond the nation-
state—provided they obey the same laws as those operating only at the national level.

The only issue that may be unique to Euro-citizenship is that of the
number of potential levels. In all federal systems, individuals and organizations have at least dual citizenship. They "belong" both to the subnational and the national states.[23] With the development of an intermediate
"regional" level of political authority and policy *compétence* in so many
member states and its gradual assertion at the level of the EU, it becomes
at least feasible to think of "four-layered" citizenship becoming possible
for many Europeans. Each of these layers—the local, the regional, the national, and the supranational—could have its (admittedly overlapping) set
of rights and obligations, regulated in a general way by the principle of
subsidiarity.[24]

CONSEQUENTIAL

There is no doubt that the acquisition of national citizenship by individuals no longer carries with it the serious consequences in terms of rights
and obligations that it once did. In contemporary Western democracies,

resident aliens are protected from most of the dangers of arbitrary and discriminatory treatment by the "state of law," and they are usually eligible for the benefits of the "state of welfare"—once they have lived there for a sufficient period and/or if they can demonstrate that they reside there legally. They can usually exercise some participatory rights, such as forming associations and petitioning authorities, although they are often denied the right to vote in elections, the right to certain forms of state employment, the obligation to serve in the armed forces (where there is still conscription), and, in the United States, the obligation to serve on juries. One indirect proof of this growing inconsequentiality would be the increasing proportion of those who are eligible to become citizens of the country in which they reside who do not even bother to attempt to do so.[25]

The consequentiality of developing European citizenship is much more problematic. The symbolic trappings are almost all there: a capital city, a flag, an anthem, a symphony orchestra, a passport, and, eventually, a driving license—but they do not bear the same meaning (and, in the last two cases, one has to pass through a national government to acquire them). Most of the TEU provisions concerning Euro-citizenship were not novel. They had already been "acquired" without much fanfare via the internal regulations of the EP or ECJ or included in various treaties sponsored by the Council of Europe. Many of them are not even exclusive to EU membership but apply to legally resident aliens and firms as well. Even if one were to assemble a list of all the rights that Euro-citizens have acquired since the EEC's founding in 1958—regardless of their source or substance—it might be difficult to convince most individuals that they had gained much that their respective national governments was not already providing.

For example, the much publicized "Four (better, Five) Freedoms" of the Single European Market—(1) freedom for the exchange of goods, (2) freedom for the movement of persons, (3) freedom of professional establishment, (4) freedom for the provision of services, and (5) freedom for the circulation of money and credit—are also, by and large, available to outsiders—thanks to GATT and other multi- or bilateral arrangements. Some of the more recent "Euro-goodies" have been more selectively provided, namely, the grants and subsidies that are being distributed under such acronyms as BRITE, JESSI, ERASMUS, LINGUA, COMMETT, and so forth. However consequential these programs may be for the individual or firm that is privileged to receive them, they do not amount to very much in the aggregate. Ironically, agricultural subsidies that are the most lucrative and broadly distributed EU payoff directly to its citizens have only succeeded in creating a deeply resentful group that seems to feel no special affection for its supranational benefactor!

What is certainly more important in the long run are the procedural/legal guarantees that Euro-citizens enjoy concerning equal treatment of women and part-time workers, better consumer and environmental protection, emergency medical care and legal help when traveling within the European Union, fair competitive practices between firms, uniform conditions for company formation, minimal health and safety standards, and protection against foreign (read American) subversion of their cultures. No matter how extensive these rights and protections are or how much they accumulate in the directives approved by the council, the regulations of the commission, and the decisions of the ECJ, these aspects of "market membership" have only an indirect impact on the quality of "political citizenship."

INDIVIDUAL

Democratic theory seems unequivocal on this issue: citizens must be individual human beings. Only an adult person capable of ethical reasoning and independent action can be expected to fulfill his or her rights and obligations. This theoretical presumption clashes with the obvious empirical fact that the relation between individual citizens and public authorities has become increasingly *organized* and *intermediated*. Participation may be individual, but effective access to decision makers depends on organizations. Communication among citizens passes increasingly through the parties, associations, and movements of which they are members or followers. Moreover, these organizations are not (and cannot be) democratically constituted. They invariably introduce interests of their own, significant distortions of citizen preference, into the political process, and they can pursue their objectives in multiple sites and over long time periods. It does not seem an exaggeration to suggest that these intermediaries have tended to displace (if not supplant) the efforts of individuals and traditional collectivities. In short, organizations have become the predominant and effective citizens of national democratic polities.[26]

Moreover, these associations and movements have already acquired "quasi-citizenship" rights at the national level. Actually, it would be more accurate to say that they have taken certain liberties with the political process because, instead of commonly defined and equally accessible rights, they have succeeded in influencing authorities on a piecemeal basis—class by class, sector by sector, profession by profession. Many have been formally recognized by national policy makers, sometimes as monopolistic organizations, and accorded regular access to their deliberations with a presumptive right to be consulted on all issues in their respective domains before binding decisions are taken.[27] Some have even received the equivalent of welfare entitlements: to financial subsidies, goods in kind, state-mandated obligatory dues, off-loaded public services, and so forth. All that is missing from this tale of gradual and uneven accumulation of organizationally privileged access is a general and systematic practice of equalizing access to these rights and obligations for all organized interests.

To the extent that size and complexity are key factors in enhancing the relative importance of organizational over individual citizens, there is every reason to expect that they will be even more influential at the level of the emerging Euro-polity. The commission seems to have recognized this from the very beginning when it deliberately encouraged and financed the formation of European-level associations.[28] It also established a procedure for recognizing their special Euro-status that implied privileged access to its deliberations, even if recognition was not always limited to only one organization per category. Each of its directorates-general soon surrounded itself with a vast number of standing, advisory and management committees, most of which were based on functional rather than territorial principles of representation.[29] Apparently, in the early stages, the commission attempted to confine lobbying to interactions with certified Euro-level associations, but this practice was subsequently relaxed to permit an increasing volume of direct contacts with national interest representatives.[30]

This structure of advisory committees and expert groups has mushroomed over the subsequent years. The commission itself has never employed very many officials[31] and has depended heavily on *comitologie*— that is, consultation with interest representatives, national government employees, and experts for both drafting its directives and monitoring compliance with them. Interest representatives are well remunerated for attending these meetings, and these payments could even be interpreted as a conscious subsidy for the development of an "appropriately structured" system of interest intermediation.

Despite these consistent efforts at promoting Euro-associations, the officials in Brussels have not been successful in establishing viable Euro-corporatist arrangements, except on a less visible and consequential sectoral ("mesocorporatist") basis.[32] As one well-informed observer has put it, "Brussels is getting closer to Washington than to Bonn, Paris or London."[33] If so, the implications for the future of the Euro-polity and its legitimacy could be quite substantial. At least on the continent, it has long been recognized that formally organized and officially recognized interest intermediaries played a key role in screening and diverting group preferences into broader class and sectoral channels and in subsequently governing the behavior of their members. These organizations permitted, even encouraged, a mode of economic production and a distribution of social benefits that was distinctive. "Organized capitalism" was the label sometimes affixed to the more extreme national versions of this, and there was every expectation that something like it would become the hallmark of supranational integration.

Instead, there is growing evidence of "disorganized capitalism" at the European Community level without the elements of official recognition, assured access, hierarchy and monopoly.[34] In such a disjointed and competitive setting, Euro-associations are not necessarily privileged interlocutors, and higher-order peak associations may not be preferred over more specialized ones. They must compete for influence with a wide variety of other units: national states, parastate corporations, subnational governments, large private firms, and even lobbyists and lawyers intervening on behalf of individual clients. The policy outcomes become less predictable; majorities become more difficult to mobilize. The power of public coercion is blunted, but so is the capacity of the state to overcome private exploitation. The most accurate appellation for this system of interest intermediation is *pluralism.*

Moreover, in the emerging Euro-polity, this trend toward supranational pluralism in both the structures of authority and the associations of interest has advanced unchecked by powerful mechanisms of territorial representation and electoral accountability—as they were previously at the national level. Whether this "Americanized" form of collective citizenship and influence wielding will be regarded as legitimate—except by the British—is a matter for serious conjecture.

MAKING SOME MODEST PROPOSALS FOR REFORM

As noted earlier, the Treaty of Maastricht and the 1996 Inter-Governmental Conference on the institutions of the European Union that led to the Treaty of Amsterdam explicitly invited actors to propose reforms in the form and substance of Euro-citizenship and eventually (contingent upon the support of the commission) to present them for the (unanimous) approval of the member states. In the light of this invitation, and with the assumption that democratizing the EU by expanding the role of Euro-citizens in its deliberations and decisions is a desirable goal, I would like to advance some "modest proposals" that might not only be feasible in the immediate future but could also produce some consequential changes.

Modest Proposal 1

There is one potential measure that would be relatively easy to implement (and perhaps even be acceptable to member national governments under present conditions) that would have a rapid and dramatic impact: *the insertion of direct referenda into the existing Euro-elections.* The EU has already had the indirect (and probably unintended) effect of encouraging its member states to make greater use of this mechanism; why not incorporate it within its own practices?[35] What if either the European Parliament by absolute majority or any group of European citizens over a certain size and distributed across a certain number of member states could place on the ballot, along with the usual lists for electing MEPs, two or three items for popular approval?[36] The number would have to be limited for practical purposes, and some mechanism would have to be set up to decide which items to favor at a given moment (the most democratic solution would be selection by lot). Even if the results of these referenda were not binding, they would almost assuredly have a considerable influence on policy makers at both the national and supranational levels. Most important, competition for yes and no votes would definitely increase public attention with regard to European issues in general and improve the *Öffentlichkeit* with which specific measures would be discussed and defended. The very fact that Euro-elections do not, by and large, coincide with national elections and that they presently involve only a rather simple choice of party candidates by closed national or regional lists (except in Great Britain until 1999) has created a potentially attractive "political opportunity space" that could be utilized at very little additional cost.[37] And, who knows — inserting referenda items on significant issues might even invert the present tendency toward declining participation.[38]

Modest Proposal 2

A second innovation would also contribute to differentiating Euro-elections from their national counterparts and serve to forge a more personal and enduring link between the Euro-voter and his or her representative to the European Parliament. Beyond the obvious need to reform nomination procedures and the constituencies within which votes are solicited and tallied (a matter I address in the next chapter), one could imagine *a dual system in which each Euro-citizen would be entitled to vote twice:* once, for his or her preferred candidate (on a national or, better, regional party list), and again, for that candidate's term of office — say, one or two terms.[39] Not only would this allow for a novel opportunity to express individual intensities of preference, but it could even promote the formation of a more stable and dedicated corps of Euro-deputies by making the position more attractive and allowing for the accumulation of expertise. Presumably, the longer-serving members of the EP would be explicitly legitimated by the electorate for this purpose, and their greater professionalism would free them of the usual dependence on national party apparatuses and political careers. One would have every reason to suspect that these "superdeputies" would devote more energy toward developing a more autonomous and active European-level party system than has heretofore been the case.

Modest Proposal 3

Following this general strategy of trying to make participation in Euro-elections more distinct from national elections, it would seem desirable that *Euro-citizens should vote over a lengthier period of time and cast their ballots by mail or, better, by electronic means.* What if Euro-citizens were given an entire week (during which polls or other projections of outcome would be prohibited) to contemplate the candidacies and the referenda items and eventually to register their preferences at their leisure—either by mailing in their votes via the traditional method for absentee balloting or by using their home computers or Minitels?[40] Information could be made available through these same instruments; fraud could be kept in check through the use of national personal identification numbers (which already exist). Traditional democratic theorists, with their fondness for the *Àgora*, will object that this eliminates the crucial element of face-to-face interaction and collective deliberation (some of which might be vicariously replaced by the development of "virtual groups" making imaginative use of the Internet—although admittedly these are not likely to form a random sample of the citizenry). Feminists might argue that voting in the home could result in male domination or appropriation of the choice process (although this probably ignores, in my opinion, the changing role of women in the workplace and underestimates the capacity of housewives for independent action). What such a reform would definitely accomplish would be to place the EU very visibly and resolutely in the forefront of technological change—something that the commission has been trying to do since the 1980s.

Modest Proposal 4

If, as argued here, what is needed for the future legitimation of EU decision making is more of an effort at distinguishing "market membership" from "political citizenship," then some more explicit and dramatic political commitment will have to be made—if only to remind Europeans that do enjoy distinctive rights and obligations as a result of their respective national polity's membership in the EU. One response has already been suggested: *the EU should subscribe to the European Convention for the Protection of Human Rights and Fundamental Freedoms and thereby make it unequivocally enforceable through the European Court of Justice.* In fact, the ECJ has already "appropriated" these rights in its jurisprudence, but the member states have so far been reluctant to place them explicitly within the *acquis communautaire*.[41]

What is likely to be much more controversial would be to succumb to the tendency to go beyond the existing convention and to include some of the so-called "third" or "fourth" generation of human rights. The most obvious candidate for inclusion might be "environmental rights" since there exist relatively high expectations that the EU should exercise greater authority in this policy arena where manifest cross-border externalities are so frequent. Other possible candidates could be women's rights, sexual rights, children's rights, and even animal rights. Needless to say, any such attempt to load up the list of items initially to be placed above and beyond the democratic process will be hotly contested and could endanger the whole effort.

Of course, in the "big bang" federalist scenario, this European Bill of Rights should be appended to a definitive constitutionalization of the entire integration process. Recognizing that nothing remotely so ambitious is likely to emerge in the near future, it might still be significant just to make a minimal symbolic gesture, especially if it were to be combined with an explicit codification of the economic and social rights that have already been acknowledged in previous EEC/EC/EU treaties and directives.

Modest Proposal 5

Another, admittedly more controversial, proposal would be to "endow" the EU with a special responsibility for defining and protecting the status of permanent residents in the member states who are neither national citizens of these states nor of any other member state of the EU. Let us call this *the creation of a special status for Euro-denizens*.[42] It would entitle those who acquired it to a uniformity of treatment within the EU with regard to the economic freedoms of trade, capital movement, personal travel, and professional establishment and whatever social entitlements and protections are negotiated between the member states, but it would not necessarily ensure that they would have equal political rights.[43]

Until now, the status of Euro-citizens has been clearly contingent upon the prior acquisition of citizenship in one of the member states, and various protocols have insisted that only national authorities have the capacity to define how this status is granted or acquired. The status of Euro-denizens has been much more ambiguous—and subject to considerable variation on a country-by-country basis. Depending on the possibilities for obtaining legal entry, permanent residence, and eventual naturalization, all member states have within their borders large numbers of "non-EU-persons"—legally or illegally residing.[44] Moreover, there is every indication that their numbers (presently estimated at fifteen million) are growing rapidly and posing ever more acute social and political problems. Given such pressures on the ill-defended and often ill-defined borders of the EU, combined with the unrestricted freedom of movement among the so-called Schengen countries, it is certainly conceivable that some member country will create a "market" in denizens—provided that its clients could be counted on to move on and establish themselves elsewhere. One could even imagine a country's selling its citizenship to foreigners who wish to live elsewhere in the European Union.[45]

The major advantage of an explicit status of Euro-denizenship would be to standardize these conditions of entry and residence and thereby preclude opportunistic practices by individual countries. It could also combine rather nicely with the embryonic efforts under Title VI of the Treaty on European Union to develop a more uniform policy on visa requirements, conditions for obtaining political asylum, and related immigration issues. I rather agree with Castro Oliveira that, in the present political climate, it is highly likely that the initial result would be "a restrictive immigration policy accompanied by some improvements in the rights of third country nationals," but it would represent a significant extension of EU *compétences* in an area of growing policy concern. Moreover, there is every indication that the creation of such a status would eventually generate spillover effects in other policy realms through the mechanisms of declarative statements and judicial interpretation.[46]

Modest Proposal 6

The European Union could, with relatively little effort and not much immediate effect, become the first polity in the world to practice *universal citizenship*—that is, to grant full rights of membership in the community from the moment of birth to all persons born within its territory or to its citizens living abroad, as well as to those children who are subsequently naturalized. Recognizing the manifest incapacity of children to exercise the formal political rights directly and independently, this reform further proposes that the parents of each child be empowered to exercise the right to vote until such time as the child reaches the age of maturity established by national law. To the best of my knowledge, the EU would be the first to accord multiple votes to adult child-raising citizens.

In line with the general objectives of making the exercise of Euro-citizenship distinctive from that of national citizenship and of ensuring that Euro-citizenship supplements and not supplants national citizenship, universal citizenship—even if vicariously exercised until maturity—would seem to have a number of political advantages:

1. It should make the emerging Euro-democracy more "future oriented." Not only would allowing children the vote constitute a symbolic recognition that the Euro-polity has a responsibility for future generations, but it would also provide a real incentive for these youngsters to develop an early interest in politics and to do so through an awareness of the importance of the European level of aggregation.

2. Precisely because of this incentive, it is to be expected that children—once they become aware of the right that their parents are exercising in their name in elections to the European Parliament—will increasingly hold their parents accountable for the way in which they distribute their electoral preferences, which, in turn, might make the parents more aware of the importance of these elections.

3. The latter point also suggests that the measure should increase various forms of intergenerational discussion about political issues and partisan orientations in general—strengthening channels of political socialization and improving elements of citizen training within the family that seem to have considerably diminished in recent decades. It may even compensate for the prodigious decline in sense of party identification at the national level and improve that at the supranational level.

4. Enfranchising children and youths will contribute to a greater equilibrium of the political process over the life cycle. With increasing life spans and a stable age of retirement, older persons have become a larger and larger component of the total citizenry, and they have both the time and financial resources to participate disproportionately in the policy process—with the result that an increasing proportion of public funds are being spent for the health and welfare of the aged and a decreasing sum on the education and training of youth. In the longer run, this is bound to be a self-defeating process as a smaller and less productive set of active workers must pay for a larger and larger set of retired workers.

5. Although I personally doubt the effect will be great, the reform might have some positive impact on the birthrate. It would even more assuredly provide a major signal of support for the integrity of the family and for "family values." Providing childbearing families with multiple votes should provide a significant incentive for politicians to pay more attention to such issues.

DRAWING SOME CONCLUSIONS ABOUT THE POTENTIAL FOR EURO-CITIZENSHIP

Europeans seem to have rapidly grown accustomed to the elements of *economic* citizenship that the EU has provided for them. Those freedoms to buy and sell goods, to invest and exchange currency, to receive and deliver services, to move personally, and to exercise one's profession across national borders are positively appreciated (and largely taken for granted), but they certainly have not generated a high level of identification with the institutions that produced them.[47] Now the question is whether the EU can graft onto these economic freedoms a new set of explicitly *political* rights and obligations that Europeans will find sufficiently appealing and consequential that they will finally (if not exclusively or definitively) come to identify with the supranational polity that protects them.

The proposals suggested here for the development of Euro-citizenship are deliberately modest. They recognize the impossibility of founding or refounding Europe *ex novo* and of simply replacing the extremely rich and complex set of symbols, identities, expectations, and affective ties that bind national citizens to their respective polities. At best, Euro-citizenship is condemned for the foreseeable future to be "supplementary"—which does not mean that its development cannot contribute the legitimization of the integration process as a whole. A great deal hinges, in my opinion, on the symbolic novelty of these new rights and obligations, as well as on the net material advantage they generate for those who enjoy them.

But, by making Euro-elections as different as possible from national ones and by recognizing the emergence of new forms of collective and generational citizenship, the promoters of an increasingly politicized integration process would be taking a calculated risk. Putative Euro-citizens will not only have to evaluate their newly acquired freedoms as *consequential* enough so that it is worth their time and effort to exercise them, but they must also recognize them as *democratic* (i.e., as capable of rendering the rulers of the Euro-polity more accountable).

The previous gamble on direct elections to the European Parliament seems, so far, to have failed on both counts. Another such failure could diminish, not strengthen, the legitimacy of the Euro-polity as a whole. This is another way of saying that modest reforms in the form and content of citizenship introduced in an isolated fashion (and, especially, if they are granted from above without any prior mobilization and struggle) are not likely to make much of a positive contribution to democratization; moreover, not all of those proposed are likely to be approved and implemented. Upon deliberation, some are bound to seem more acceptable than others. And those that are found most acceptable are likely to prove least consequential—at least in the short run.

So, we must not expect too much from Euro-citizenship. Alone, it is definitely not the panacea that will resolve the EU's rising problems with legitimacy. Even if all of the aforementioned advocated reform measures were approved and implemented, their effect would be only gradual and marginal. What is required if the process of European integration is to shift from a logic of functional interdependencies to one of politicized exchanges is a broader package of reforms—however modest the individual elements—not just in the scope of citizenship but also in its forms of representation and its rules of decision making. Chapters 3 and 4 will take up the challenge of identifying *que faire?* in these two dimensions.

AN EXCURSUS ON SOCIAL CITIZENSHIP IN THE EU

Compared to the resounding (if rather vacuous) commitment in the Treaty of Maastricht to political citizenship, the EU has made only fitful and erratic progress in defining its social citizenship. No one should be surprised that there is so little "Social Europe." If anything, the absence of any substantial commitment by the members of the EU to harmonize, or even to coordinate, their social policies is overdetermined. So many objective features of what Europe is not (at least, not yet) combine with several subjective aspects of the conjuncture in which Europeans are presently living that it is highly unlikely that much progress will be made in this domain for the foreseeable future.

First, the member states are at different levels of economic development. Their factors of production operate at systematically different levels of efficiency and relative scarcity; hence, they command different levels of income and return on investment. Variations in the social charges, tax regimes, and formalities surrounding these different points of departure are important elements in determining the competitiveness of those striving to "catch up."

Second, the member states have acquired over the past hundred years or more quite diverse "packets" of social policies and (especially) ways of financing them; moreover, their mass publics seem relatively firmly (if begrudgingly) committed to their respective national status quos—at least in the sense that they collectively resist reductions in the benefits to which they have become "entitled."

Third, the interest associations that have grown up around (and also within) national social policy regimes, as well as the general systems of industrial relations, vary considerably among member states. These organizations (especially trade unions) are notoriously resilient to change, and many of their key financial and political resources are tied to the role they play in the national institutions of social policy.

Fourth, the influence of neoliberal ideology with its hostility to state intervention in general and preference for privatized insurance schemes in particular has spread unevenly across member states and remains a salient issue of dispute within them.

Fifth, even if these items could be overcome, the EU itself is not close to becoming a sovereign state with its own legitimate powers of enforcement and taxation and hence limited both by its dependence on member states for the implementation of whatever social policies would be decided and by the reluctance of these polities to provide it with the funds necessary for any positive effort at redistribution or compensation.

Finally, the system of representation that has emerged *pari passu* with the European integration process has provided privileged access and accountability to business interests and ineffectual incentives for the organization of "policy takers," making it more difficult for workers, pensioners, consumers, patients, students, and the impoverished to articulate their demands at the supranational level. The European Parliament, where such demands might predictably be expected to focus, has only a limited power of budgetary review and virtually no capacity to determine the policy agenda. As long as there is no "balance of class forces" and no "effective party system" surrounding the definition of social citizenship at the European level, and as long as capitalists are convinced that such a commitment is not in their interests, there is virtually no chance that major substantive policies will be enacted.

If all this were not enough, monetary unification and the impending prospect of eastern enlargement will only make the situation worse by introducing new elements of social inequality into this embryonic polity!

The fact that so little has been accomplished so far does not mean that nothing can be accomplished in the near future. It just means that, strategically, one should proceed *à petits pas* (as Jean Monnet would have put it) and that, tactically, one should take advantage of emerging "opportunity structures" (as Sidney Tarrow would say). The latter is provided by the impending disruptions of monetary unification and eastern enlargement; the former could be fulfilled by what I shall call "a Euro-stipendium."

A Less Modest Proposal (Number 7) for Social Citizenship

The European Union should declare as one of its basic purposes the elimination of extreme poverty within its borders. Since most of its member states have already recognized this objective explicitly and many of them have national programs for this purpose in effect, the major innovation would be to "Europeanize" the commitment—both by basing it on a Europe-wide statistical calculation and creating a unique fund to finance it. The means for doing this would consist of a *Euro-stipendium*—that is, the monthly payment of a stipulated amount of euros to all citizens or legal permanent residents (denizens) living within the EU whose total earnings correspond to less than one-third of the average income of everyone living within the EU. By standard convention, those falling in this category are classified as "in extreme poverty."

Eventually, the total sum of expenditures for this purpose could be set at a figure approximately corresponding to the present combined value of all EU agricultural subsidies and regional/structural funds. In the interim, it could be set at some proportion of that amount, with the understanding that over a stipulated period of time, this would rise gradually to replace existing EU programs of sectoral and regional redistribution. The total yearly amount of the individual stipendium would be adjusted according, on the one hand, to the funds made available and, on the other, to the total number of persons deemed eligible so that, in no case, would they exceed a predetermined level of expenditure—even in the event of enlargement in the number of member countries. In other words, provided it were possible to shift the basis of EU "welfare" from payments to agricultural enterprises for producing (or not producing) specific crops and from grants to the governments of designed subnational regions for coming up with plausible development projects to simple money transfers to individuals, the aggregate cost to the EU and its member countries would be zero!

Needless to say, an immediate shift in the *destinataires* of existing funds is not likely to be politically feasible—either because the group interests affected have sufficient clout to prevent a negative redistribution of the EU funds to which they have become "entitled," or because the national and subnational governments involved would receive significantly less of the *juste retour* than they have become accustomed to receive from the EU. It should be possible to "fine-tune" the initiative during an intermediate period so that farmers could become eligible at a lower threshold (say, at one-half rather than one-third of the EU average income) and that (allegedly) underdeveloped regions and countries might be compensated for not having enough people living in extreme poverty. Nothing should be done, however, to sustain any longer than is absolutely necessary the substantial welfare benefits that presently go to wealthy and productive agricultural enterprises and to consultants and other intermediaries involved in inventing reasons for spending regional/structural funds. And, it is important for symbolic reasons that the amount of the Euro-stipendium be the same throughout the EU and that it be based not on national income distributions but on the distribution of income at the level of EU member countries as a whole.

Not only would such a policy be much easier and less costly to administer than the existing ones, but it would also distribute benefits directly to targeted individuals—who, incidentally, have a high propensity for immediate consumption of relatively labor-intensive goods and services and, hence, who would generate lots of aggregate demand and additional employment. Moreover, they would do so on a continuing basis since the Euro-stipendium would continue to be paid regularly, as long as individuals remained eligible.

The political context that makes this "immodest" proposal especially appealing at this moment is formed, first, by monetary unification and, subsequently, by eastern enlargement. One predictable effect of a single European currency and interest rate will be increasing income disparities within member countries. The present policy of structural/regional funds is much too rigid to cope with such an eventuality—especially if the increased inequalities at the margin are not concentrated in areas already designed for such funds. The Euro-stipendium would ensure that all those dramatically and negatively affected would be protected, and it is not tied to any fixed territorial criterion. Those who slipped into extreme poverty as an indirect and unintended consequence of monetary unification would be protected no matter where they lived and no matter whether others in their vicinity were similarly affected. Moreover, the compensation would be automatic and not necessitate the (time-consuming, costly, and politically contingent) intervention of price-setting committees or project mongers.

But the major appeal stems from the anticipated impact of eastern enlargement. Everyone recognizes that the existing EU welfare policies of agricultural subsidies and regional grants cannot simply be extended eastward—without very substantial and politically discriminatory modifications. The sheer fact that all of the immediate candidates have per-capita incomes lower than that of the lowest existing member state (Greece) cannot be ignored. Average income in euros is bound to decline with their entry, which, of course, would be automatically reflected in the calculation of the Euro-stipendium. By eliminating (or sharply redefining) the existing programs before eastern enlargement and by defining ex ante a total sum to be used to alleviate poverty within the EU as a whole, one could set the initial levels of the stipendium at an acceptable aggregate cost—and, then, extend it in the future simultaneously and proportionately as the necessity arises, as experience with the program accumulates, and as dispositions for solidarity within the EU change.

NOTES

1. Or, as Marshall put it, "the right to share to the full in the social heritage and to live the life of a civilized being according to the standards prevailing in the society." *Citizenship and Social Class* (Cambridge: Cambridge University Press, 1950), 11.

2. "Citizenship and Beyond: The Social Dynamics of an Idea," *Social Research* 41, no. 4 (Winter 1974): 683.

3. Significantly, the TEU only mentions rights and protections. It offers not a word or hint about obligations or duties.

4. "Traditions of Nationhood and Politics of Citizenship," Social Science Research Council (New York), *States and Social Structures Newsletter* 9 (Winter 1989): 4–8.

5. "Traditions of Nationhood," p. 5.

6. Although as Michael Walzer notes, citizens may still be compelled "to live for the state" since national laws typically prohibit and punish suicide. *Obligations: Essays on Disobedience, War, and Citizenship* (Cambridge, Mass.: Harvard University Press, 1970), 77–98. I would add that the current evolution of American legal doctrine and public policy seems to be aimed at compelling its citizens "to procreate for the state" by making abortion increasingly difficult to obtain.

7. The recent controversy in the United States over the burning of the flag suggests that the issue is far from over—at least in that most patriotic of advanced industrial societies.

8. This raises the delicate issue of whether there is a functional substitute for mass mobilization and actual combat. The Cold War certainly enhanced the sacred image of the "Western world" for several postwar generations. In its absence, ideologues have tried to replace it with an alleged "clash of civilizations" and, more specifically, with the "green menace" of Islamic fundamentalism. So far, this has not proven very credible. For example, any attempt to get the EU or the WEU to espouse the French policy of unconditional support for the Algerian military dictatorship against its fundamentalist enemies would seem more likely to divide than unify contemporary Europe.

9. I am indebted to several conversations with and the reading of several unpublished papers by Karl-Heinz Reif, head of the commission's Survey Research Unit in Brussels, for this (and many other) observations. For a very comprehensive and path-breaking analysis of popular attitudes in Europe toward the EU, see *Public Opinion and Internationalized Governance,* ed. Oskar Niedermayer and Richard Sinnott (Oxford: Oxford University Press, 1995). For a more recent analysis of the downward trend, see R. Sinnott and N. Winston, "Disintegrative Tendencies in EU Public Opinion," paper for the ECPR Joint Sessions, Oslo, 1996.

10. Anyone who doubts this or believes that it has completely disappeared should watch the hilarious movie *Die Schweizermacher.*

11. This is not to say that there are not those who have considered such a trend alarming. In the United States, the struggle against multiculturalism and in favor of imposing English as the legally exclusive language of the country are clear signs of a reaction against the "denationalization" of membership in the American polity.

12. It should also be pointed out that despite all the talk of Euro-citizenship, in order to enjoy its benefits one must first be a national citizen of one of its member countries—and these countries are (so far) exclusively responsible for setting the criteria under which this status can be acquired by foreigners. Needless to say, the national rules concerning naturalization remain very diverse.

The TEU is very clear that no independent European citizenship is being created or even contemplated. Its Article F(1) strongly commits the EU to respecting the national identities of its member states. For the benefit of the doubting Danes, the European Council meeting in Birmingham repeated that the rights and protections of citizenship in the EU do not in any way take the place of national citizenship. *Bulletin EC* 10-1992, pt. I.8: 9.

Nevertheless, Gérard-René de Groot has shown that in analogous historical situations (the German Empire, Switzerland, and the United States), it eventually became imperative that the central authority establish some common rules and degree of control. "The Relationship between the Nationality of the Member-States of the European Union and European Citizenship," paper presented at the EUI European Forum Conference on European Citizenship: An Institutional Challenge, Florence, June 13–15, 1996.

13. This seems close to what Jürgen Habermas has called *Verfassungspatriotismus*. For a more complete discussion of his views on the possibility of nonethnic, nonnational citizenship, see his "Citizenship and National Identity: Some Reflections on the Future of Europe," in *Theorizing Citizenship,* ed. Ronald Beiner (Albany: State University of New York Press, 1995), 255–82. Jean-Marc Ferry and Paul Thibaud have engaged in a fascinating intergenerational debate in which the latter takes the traditional (one is tempted to say French) position that nationality and citizenship cannot be severed from each other, and the former defends this possibility (*Discussion sur l'Europe* [Paris: Calmann-Lévy, 1992]). Also see Jean-Marc Ferry, "Identité et citoyenneté européennes" in *L'Europe au soir du siècle: Identité et démocratie,* ed. Jacques Lenoble and Nicole Dewandre (Paris: Esprit, 1992).

14. *Strukturwandel der Öffentlichkeit* (Frankfurt: Suhrkamp, 1990).

15. See, for example, Enid Lakeman, "Elections to the European Parliament, 1989," *Parliamentary Affairs* 43 (January 1990), where the EP elections are treated as mere extensions of national elections—hence the notion developed by Karl-Heinz Reif that these elections are condemned to be "second-order": "Nine Second-Order National Elections," *European Journal of Political Research* 8 (1980): 3–45, 145–62. Also, J. Lodge and V. Herman, *Direct Elections to the European Parliament: A Supranational Perspective* (London: Macmillan, 1982).

16. Karl-Heinz Reif, *Ten European Elections* (Aldershot, England: Glower, 1985).

17. The right of individuals to address the European Parliament or to bring cases before the European Court of Justice was already written into their respective internal regulations—and is not restricted to nationals of EC/EU member states. It seems that the right to petition the new ombudsman is also open to third-country nationals who reside in member states.

18. For a general discussion of the issue, see Juliet Lodge, "Transparency and Democratic Legitimacy," *Journal of Common Market Studies* 32 (1994): 343–68.

19. Juliet Lodge, "Democracy in the EU: The Interrelationship between Supra-national, National and Subnational Levels of Government," in *Démocratie et construction européenne,* ed. Mario Telò (Brussels: Éditions de l'Université de Bruxelles, 1995), 238–50. Also see her earlier article, cited in n. 18.

20. Philippe C. Schmitter and Wolfgang Streeck, "Organized Interests and the Europe of 1992," in *Political Power and Social Change: The United States Faces the United Europe,* ed. N. J. Ornstein and M. Perlman (Washington, D.C.: AEI Press, 1991), 46–67; Franz Traxler and Philippe C. Schmitter, "Perspektiven Europäischer Integration, verbandlicher Interessenintermediation und Politikfor-mulierung," in *Europäische Integration und verbandliche Interessenintermediation,* ed. V. Eichener and H. Voelzkow (Marburg: Metropolis, 1994), 45–71; Franz Traxler and Philippe C. Schmitter, "The Emerging Euro-Polity and Orga-nized Interests," *European Journal of International Relations* 1, no. 2 (June 1995): 191–218.

21. Andrew McLaughlin and Justin Greenwood, "The Management of Interest Representation in the European Union," *Journal of Common Market Studies* 33, no. 1 (March 1995): 143–56.

22. Gary Marks, François Nielsen, Leonard Ray, and Jane Salk, "Competencies, Cracks and Conflicts: Regional Mobilization in the European Union," in *Gover-nance in the European Union,* ed. G. Marks et al. (London: Sage, 1996), 40–63.

23. In the extreme case of Switzerland, they are also deeply engaged in mem-bership at the communal as well as the cantonal and federal levels. So layered is the process that voting turnout tends to be higher in communal elections than in cantonal ones, and in cantonal than federal ones. In fact, in that country, natural-ization first involves one's becoming a member of a commune and canton before acquiring the status of a Swiss national.

24. For an argument in this sense, see André Berten, "Identité européenne, une ou multiple?" in *L'Europe au soir du,* ed. Lenoble and Dewandre.

25. I know of no hard and firm data on this subject, time-series or cross-sec-tional, and would appreciate anyone's calling my attention to where I could find them. My impression, based on the places I have lived in recent years, is that the proportion of denizens has tended to increase, but I would be the first to admit that this is hardly a representative sample. Note that a rival explanation for this (unproven) fact might be that more and more of the foreigners resident in ad-vanced industrial societies believe that they will eventually return (or be allowed to return) to their country of origin.

26. The only person so far courageous enough to suggest such an eventuality and to place it in a published title has been, appropriately, a Scandinavian: Johan P. Olsen, *Organized Democracy* (Oslo: Universitetsforlaget, 1983).

27. *Vernehmlassungsverfahren* is the untranslatable Swiss term for this.

28. For example, Sicco Mansholt seems to have played a major role in the founding of the peak association of European farmers, COPA. Leon Lindberg and Stuart Scheingold, *Europe's Would-Be Polity* (Upper Saddle River, N.J.: Prentice Hall, 1970), 173. Other Commission officials helped found BEUC for consumers, according to Dusan Sidjanski and Ural Ayberk, "Le Nouveau visage des groupes d'intérêt communautaires," *Revue d'intégration européenne* 10 (1987): 180. In the extreme case of EUROFER, the EC deliberately sponsored the creation of a

regional cartel. See Alan Butt Philip, "Pressure Groups in the European Community," *UACES Occasional Papers* 2 (1985): 45.

29. It should be stressed that access to these committees is not restricted to functional interest representatives. Many involve designated "experts" in the processes of decision making and implementation, although these may often be difficult to distinguish from interest spokespersons. For a description of forty-six of these consultative bodies, see Economic and Social Committee of the European Communities, *Community Advisory Committees for the Representation of Socio-Economic Interests* (Farnborough: Saxon, 1980).

30. See, in addition to Sidjanski and Aybeck, "Le Nouveau visage," James A. Caporaso, *The Structure and Function of European Integration* (Pacific Palisades, Calif.: Goodyear, 1974), 23–52.

31. Current estimates suggest approximately seventeen thousand employees, a number that includes a very large number of interpreters and other staff personnel. Exercising policy functions, there is probably no more than fifteen hundred Eurocrats, although it should be observed that they are supplemented by an even larger number of national civil servants and interest association functionaries who are seconded for various periods of time to Brussels. Also, the commission contracts out for much of its research.

32. See the articles by Schmitter and Streeck and Traxler and Schmitter cited in n. 20.

33. Wyn Grant, talk on "Business Interests in a New Europe," Center for European Studies, Stanford University, Calif., February 7, 1990.

34. See Scott Lash and John Urry, *The End of Organized Capitalism* (Cambridge: Polity, 1987).

35. Referenda seem a particularly appropriate device for dealing with issues that cannot be processed in a "normal" fashion by political parties and legislatures because they cut across the usual preferences of their members/voters. Since it is manifestly the case that many of Europe's most venerable parties are badly split internally on issues involving the concession of more or less authority to the EU, it should be appealing to their politicians to off-load responsibility to a referendum, rather than risk increasingly acrimonious factionalism.

36. One obvious place to start this process would be to submit whatever agreement is eventually reached in the forthcoming intergovernmental conference on the revision of EU institutions to such an advisory referendum. My hunch is that, if the participants during 2000 were aware that their results would be submitted to such popular scrutiny, they would be immediately compelled to expand their agenda. By confining it (as presently announced) to the so-called "leftovers" from the Treaty of Amsterdam, they would risk having to confront massive abstention since nothing excites Euro-citizens less than complex (and probably heavily compromised) agreements among states on obscure aspects of weighted voting, numbers of commissioners, and so forth.

37. It is important that Euro-elections continue to be separated from national ones, although tying them to local or provincial contests may occasionally be necessary (and have some impact on voter turnout).

38. For a more ambitious proposal along these lines, see *Transnationale Demokratie. Impulse für ein demokratische verfasstes Europa,* ed. Roland Erne, An-

dreas Gross, Bruno Kaufmann, and Heinz Kleger (Zurich: Realotopia, 1995). Fritz Scharpf in a single sentence in a footnote has summarily dismissed the idea of Euro-referenda on the grounds that such devices are only appropriately applied with a homogeneous *demos*—which is manifestly not the case of the EU. In my opinion, this involves a basic misunderstanding of how referenda have functioned historically. At the time they were introduced in Switzerland (the latter part of the nineteenth century), that country had anything but a homogeneous *demos*. At first, it was used cautiously and infrequently just for that reason. It did, indeed, reveal some very substantial differences in preference that correlated with basic religious and linguistic cleavages. However, over time, these tended to diminish. It could even be argued that the increasing frequency of recourse to referenda in that country made a significant contribution to creating a more homogeneous *demos* (and to help to stabilize its otherwise very fragmented party system). Stretching a point, I might even be prepared to make the same argument for California! See "Economic Integration, Democracy and the Welfare State," *Journal of European Public Policy* 4, no. 1 (March 1997), fn. 2.

39. Were this change to be introduced, the normal term of office (now five years and, arguably, too long) would have to be reduced to, say, three years. What might emerge within the same chamber would be a "senator" and "deputy" status differentiation in which those elected for two terms would have a putative claim on preference in committee assignments and leadership positions. Frankly, I have not considered whether this would be a desirable development, but I am convinced that enhancing the career orientation and professionalism of MEPs is a good thing from the point of view of Euro-democracy—pace the traditionally democratic assumption that politicians should be amateurs.

40. A recent experiment with mailed ballots in the U.S. state of Oregon resulted in a very significant increase in the rate of turnout.

41. For a concise description of how the ECJ managed to "appropriate" the theme of protection of human rights, see Federico G. Mancini, "The Making of a Constitution for Europe," in *The New European Community,* ed. R. Keohane and S. Hoffmann (Boulder, Colo.: Westview, 1991), 177–94.

A recent decision of the European Court of Justice (2/94 of March 28, 1996) has declared that the EU cannot simply accede to the European Convention for the Protection of Human Rights and Fundamental Freedoms, but would have to do so via an amendment to the TEU. *Financial Times,* April 16, 1996, p. 12.

42. My thoughts on this subject have been triggered by reading Alvaro Castro Oliveira, "Resident Third Country Nationals: Is It Too Early to Grant Them Union Citizenship?" paper presented at the EUI, European Forum Conference on European Citizenship: An Institutional Challenge, Florence, June 13–15, 1996.

43. According to Castro Oliveira, denizens already enjoy certain social and educational rights under EU legislation, and their survivors are guaranteed benefits from national social security systems. They do not, however, enjoy freedom of movement or establishment in any country other than the one that has granted them permanent residence.

As for political rights, there are some polities (e.g., Sweden and the canton of Neuchâtel) that already permit resident aliens to vote in local elections, and there is even an evolving set of national court decisions and resolutions of the Council of Europe that have sought to extend this as a basic human/civic right.

44. In the Italian press, these persons are often referred to as *extracomunitari*, a sort of euphemism for undesirables and alleged criminals from Albania and Africa.

45. Something approaching this situation presently exists in the relation between Portugal and Macao. Large numbers of Hong Kong residents, denied citizenship by the United Kingdom, are buying property in Macao and thereby acquiring Portuguese nationality, which they presumably can use in the future to enter, reside, and work in the United Kingdom. Analogous loopholes also permit descendents of Spanish, Portuguese, Italian, and Irish emigrants to "recuperate" the nationality of their ancestors—and live wherever they please in the EU.

46. For instance, a joint Declaration against Racism and Xenophobia adopted in 1986 by the European Parliament, the Council of Ministers and the Commission affirms their resolve "to protect the individuality and dignity of every member of society and to reject any form of segregation of foreigners." If this sort of "cheap talk" were eventually to be taken seriously by either politicians or judges, it could have far-reaching—if unintended—implications.

47. Ernst B. Haas expected this when he defined political integration as "the process whereby political actors in several distinct national settings are persuaded to shift their loyalties, expectations and political activities toward a new centre, whose institutions possess or demand jurisdiction over the pre-existing states." See *The Uniting of Europe* (Stanford, Calif.: Stanford University Press, 1958), 16.

3

Representation

As befits a large-scale, multilevel, and socially diverse polity, the EU already relies heavily on several channels of political representation. Member states in the Council of Ministers, national political parties in the European Parliament, selected functional interests in the Economic and Social Committee, and, most recently, subnational territorial units in the Committee of Regions are formally present in its decision-making processes. Informally, many classes, sectors, professions, and causes have organized themselves at the level of Europe and found their way to Brussels, Luxembourg, or Strasbourg, along with a steadily increasing phalanx of national interest associations, multinational corporations, and transnational law firms. Some of these representatives are explicitly weighted according to the size of their respective constituencies; others depend exclusively on the voluntary efforts and relative intensities of their members. Some have the right to participate with "voice and vote" in the making of binding decisions; some are invited by EU authorities to enter the obscure corridors of *comitologie* where the projects for eventually binding decisions are drafted; still others resort to less formal ways of exercising their influence in the corridors and lobbies.

All this conforms to the generic nature of modern political democracies, each of which has a very complex set of institutions involving multiple channels of representation and sites for authoritative decision making. The exercise of citizenship, whatever its level, scope, or content, is not confined to voting periodically in elections. It also can be expressed by influencing the selection of candidates; joining parties, associations, or movements; petitioning or pressuring authorities; participating in the drafting of legislation; engaging in "unconventional" protests; and so forth. Nor is the accountability of authorities only guaranteed through the traditional mechanisms of territorial constituency, partisan competition, and legislative process. Much of it can circumvent these mechanisms and focus directly through functional channels and bargaining processes on elected or appointed officials within the administrative-cum-executive apparatus of the state.

The problem with the EU, therefore, lies not in the absence of representation but in the systematically skewed distribution of the interests and passions that do manage to find their way into its complex and secretive decision-making process. From its origins, the integration process tended to privilege two sets of interests: first and formally, those of the governments of member states (with their so-called "national interests") and, second and informally, those of the business sectors most directly affected by its functional policy domains. This left out many citizens of Europe whose individual and collective well-being was indirectly, gradually, and often surreptitiously affected by EU policies: (1) large and diffuse quasi-groups of "policy takers" within each member state such as wage earners, unemployed persons, women, consumers, pensioners, youth, and so on; (2) intense and compact movements committed to some specific cause or the provision of some particular public good such as environmental protection, abortion rights, conscientious objection, and international solidarity; (3) inhabitants of subnational political units—regions, provinces, communes, municipalities—who do not feel adequately represented by their respective national governments; and (4), most importantly for the future of the integration process, transnational or cross-border coalitions of any of the preceding three categories. Whatever the formula applied, if the Euro-polity is to democratize its multiple channels of representation, it must provide greater incentives for the collective articulation and the access of these systematically underrepresented interests and passions.

Exactly what these incentives should be hinges very much on the type of polity that is emerging at the level of the European Union. If it were merely a *confederatio*, the issue would scarcely arise and attention could be focused exclusively on improving forms of collective action and accountability within the respective national polities. As a purely intergovernmental organization with easy entry and exit and with unanimity as its predominant decision rule, a confederal EU could coexist comfortably with democratic member states. If it were to become a suprastate *federatio*, most of one's attention would be focused on the formation of a European-level party system sufficiently anchored in citizen perceptions, an electoral mechanism that was uniform, reliable (and acceptable) enough to produce winning candidates and eventual governments, and an institutional arrangement that could ensure that decisions binding on the public would be held accountable to properly elected representatives and implemented uniformly and fairly by EU authorities.[1]

But if the (medium-term) problem is to design a more democratic form of representation for either a *consortio* or a *condominio*, then it may be necessary to use more imagination. The central issue revolves around the "peculiarity" that members of the Euro-polity may have different rights and obligations (in the former mode) and also be constituted by different countries (in the latter mode). Moreover, there would be no clear hierarchy of institutions that would exercise sovereignty and hence provide the focus for ultimate accountability—just a complex network of multilayered bargaining between organizations with overlapping jurisdictions. If this functional and territorial variation were only temporary (i.e., because of explicitly provisional *dérogations*), the problem would eventually eliminate itself, and those who are full members might not object to partial members enjoying "voice and vote" even in matters to which they had not (yet) accepted an equal commitment. Or, if one could be certain that Euro-sovereignty would eventually assert itself, the usual federalist mechanisms of equal status for participants, territorially differentiated powers, checks and balances, constitutional review, and supremacy of federal law should suffice.

However, in the scenario of an indefinite and perhaps permanent diversity within European institutions—and, even more especially, in an eventual *condominio* with its "eccentric" configuration of multiple Europes, each with its own functions and set of members—democratization will hinge on inventing more appropriate ways of representing citizen interests and passions.

Let us take a brief look in the following sections at what some of these inventions might be.

Modest Proposal 8

Let us first assume that, regardless of eventual variation in their commitment with regard to specific functional domains and territorial boundaries, all the countries that join the EU (or any part of it) voluntarily accept to submit themselves to a minimum common denominator of obligations and hence to the supranational authority of the commission and the Court of Justice in these (restricted) matters. This hard core of obligations would presumably incorporate key aspects of the present *acquis communautaire*, but it should be the subject of explicit negotiations and limits with regard to eventual expansion so that "partial/peripheral" participants can feel secure from "creeping entanglements" in the future. While it would certainly be a mistake to attempt to produce a *Kompetenzkatalog* based on subsidiarity that would fix the distribution of functional *compétences* and institutional jurisdictions (as is the case in most federalist systems), some kind of distinction between "primary" obligations and "secondary" commitments would be indispensable. If I am not mistaken, something like this was negotiated during the formation of the European Economic Area. Needless to say, to accommodate the special situations of the eastern applicants, it will be necessary to include apposite temporal *dérogations*—even for primary obligations and for much longer periods of time.[2]

Acceptance of this common denominator would entitle all of the signatory states—perhaps as many as thirty-five or more of them, depending on what happens to the parts from the former Yugoslavia—to representation in the European Parliament. There seems to be general agreement that the size of this body should be limited, in the interests of efficiency, to approximately seven hundred deputies. Both this cap and common political sense preclude the distribution of seats in the basis of absolute population size. My proposal would be to apply a standard formula, with room for minor modifications to guarantee at least one seat for each country and to round off fractions (it would be difficult to seat 1.75 or 13.38 deputies). Each country would be entitled to a number of members of European Parliament (MEPs) roughly proportionate to the logged value of its population. This could be called *proportionately proportional representation* and has the virtue of being relatively close to the formula currently in use for votes in the Council and seats in the EP. Admittedly, the eventual adhesion of ministates such as Andorra, San Marino, and Liechtenstein (should they apply) could bias the representation even more against large states, since each would merit at least one seat. Perhaps some form of rotational representation could be devised for those countries that do not reach a prespecified minimum threshold. In any case, each time new members would be admitted, it would be necessary to make a proportionate downward adjustment in the allocation of seats among existing members to keep the total within reasonable bounds—something that might have interesting effects on both the nomination and electoral processes. Needless to say, all MEPs, regardless of the size of their constituency and the scope of their commitment to the integration process, would be entitled to participate with equal "voice and vote"—but, as we shall now see, only in the plenary sessions of the European Parliament.

Modest Proposal 9

This is where *functionally differentiated representation* should come in. The effective legislative activity of the EP would be delegated to standing committees—with at least one assigned to monitor and render accountable the activities of each of the EU's policy domains (e.g., one for Monetary Europe, one for Agricultural Europe, another for Energy Europe, yet another for the "Schengen" Europe of Internal Security or the "Trevi" group on police cooperation, etc.). Only those countries that had accepted the full *acquis* in that specific domain would be eligible to participate in the deliberations and make the binding decisions of its corresponding committee. In effect, the EP as a whole would meet only for limited ceremonial occasions, for the approval of major rule changes and for the accession of new members. Most of the actual deliberation and decision making would take place in a series of "functional subparliaments" whose decisions would be automatically given the imprimatur of the parliament as a whole.[3]

A rules committee—elected by the EP plenary—would assign draft legislation to the appropriate committee or committees.[4] Some form of appeal procedure would have to be established to allow both members and nonmembers of the specialized committees to have something to say with regard to resolving the inevitable externalities generated between policy domains and quarrels between competing agencies. For example, if a certain proportion of the MEPs—say, one-third of the total—objected either to excessive "free-riding" by those who were not committed to joint policy making in a specific domain or to excessive provision of "selective goods" by those who were, the plenary could be empowered to come up with appropriate regulations or compensatory measures. In addition, the fact that all members recognize the general jurisdiction and principles of the ECJ should permit that institution to play a role in mediating interfunctional disputes, as well as the interstate ones they have more typically had to deal with.

Modest Proposal 10

These changes in parliamentary representation and procedure seem (to me) appropriate adjustments to make—given the increasing disparities between territorial scope and functional domain that are likely to characterize the emerging Euro-polity—but they would do little to resolve the more fundamentally democratic problem of systematic under- and overrepresentation of certain interests and passions. To correct for this, it would be desirable in the long run to modify the constituencies that the MEPs represent and the conditions under which they are nominated to compete for these positions of representation. Needless to say, this will be no easy matter in the short run since contemporary MEPs—not to mention even better-entrenched national politicians—benefit considerably from existing rules that ensure three things: (1) that most Euro-deputies are elected by PR from closed lists representing the country as a whole (except in Great Britain where a first-past-the-post system prevailed until the last Euro-elections, and Germany, Belgium, Ireland, and Italy where there are multimember regional lists);[5] (2) that control over nominations to these lists lies exclusively in the hands of national party directorates; (3) that funds to pay for campaigning in Euro-elections are paid directly (and unaccountably) to these same directorates. Under these conditions, subnational and cross-national constituencies only get represented "by accident."

Ideally, Euro-citizens should be given some direct say in the nomination process, through either local party caucuses or primaries, but this is rarely observed in the national politics of member states and would be even more difficult to implement at the supranational level where partisan identities and organizational structures are much weaker.[6] With so little possibility for their participation in the nomination process, attention has been focused almost exclusively on expanding the electoral role of Euro-citizens. For example, it has been suggested that they be accorded the opportunity to vote twice in each election, once by simple majority for individual candidates in subnational constituencies and again by proportional representation for closed lists established by transnational political parties.[7] This has the virtue of resembling a well-established (if not always well-understood) procedure followed by one of the EU member states, the Federal Republic of Germany, but it seems unlikely that such a far-reaching change would be accepted unanimously by the others—which, after all, would have to be the case under the existing rules of the council. If these countries cannot even agree on a much simpler common electoral procedure, how can one expect them to agree on something that would so dramatically empower transnational parties that barely exist?

I propose something more modest—indeed, so modest that it might initially be implemented by simple majority vote of the EP under its present rules. What if the existing European party formations in the EP were given control over one-half of the EU electoral funds allotted for each member state? And what if these funds were distributed in support of national lists in which one-half of the candidates would be nominated by these very same, admittedly embryonic and often fragmented, parliamentary parties?[8] Would this be enough to bring out latent voter preference for candidates with more transnational connections and appeals? Would national party oligarchies find it increasingly desirable to place candidates with more Euro-experience higher on their lists and become more reluctant to use it as a place to park their failed or retiring brethren? Would politicians, especially if they had the possibility of serving longer terms in the EP, come to attach their professional expectations more securely to that level of aggregation?

If it could be demonstrated on this reduced scale that such candidacies and campaigns are viable, then it might become feasible to consider eventually more consequential reforms such as creating subnational or explicitly cross-national constituencies (with either single member districts or smaller PR pools),[9] double lists and voting for national and European candidates, strictly uniform procedures for nomination and vote assignment, even additional financial and legal incentives for the formation of supranational party identities and structures independent of national ones.[10] But this is for the distant future. In the meantime, just increasing the proportion of funds controlled by Euro-parties at each successive Euro-election should provide a badly needed impetus for change—and might even generate some desirable side effects.

Modest Proposal 11

Modifying the channels of EU representation in the ways indicated here (especially if coupled with the changes I have already proposed in citizenship and those I will subsequently suggest in decision-making rules) should provide significant incentives for the expression of transnational and even subnational territorial interests—without suppressing the well-established centrality of national ones. It would, however, do little or nothing to correct the second great source of over- and underrepresentation in the Euro-polity (i.e., its functional bias in favor of business and, to a lesser extent, professional interests).

This is, of course, a bias that is not unique to the EU. In all national liberal democracies, one major problem with the "interest group chorus" is that it sings in an upper-class accent—to use the imagery that E. E. Schattschneider coined in 1960.[11] Wolfgang Streeck and I have argued that the EU is a rather extreme case of weakness in the self-organization of larger scale and more diffuse interests such as workers, women, consumers, patients, the unemployed, and pensioners[12]—not to mention the difficulties that passionate causes such as environmental protection, international solidarity, abortion rights, and feminism have encountered in articulating themselves at this level.

After first reflecting on this issue at the national level, I have subsequently concluded that a particular set of reforms in the system of financing interest associability might produce equally or even more beneficial results at the supranational level.[13] The core of what I propose consists of three, closely interrelated reforms in the nature of liberal (i.e., voluntary and individual) interest associability:

1. the establishment of a semipublic status for interest associations and social movements,
2. the financing of these associations through compulsory contributions, and
3. the distribution of these funds by means of citizen vouchers.

In the case of the EU, only associations and movements that were "European" in nature (i.e., had members and some degree of organization in several European countries) could acquire the semipublic status. They would have to agree to obey a common set of norms and submit themselves potentially to the jurisdiction of the ECJ (as well as be prepared to operate within the legal norms of whatever member country they might find themselves in). The financing of these representative organizations would come from designated EU funds—much as the present subsidies and contracts do—but receipt of these funds would not preclude their also receiving funds from national governments, private organizations, or individual persons. And the voucher system would be run in tandem with the holding of Euro-elections, alongside voting for MEPs and in eventual Euro-referenda.

The most obviously analogous reforms at the national level have been the provision of public funding for political parties and the extension of guarantees that accused persons will be provided with adequate legal counsel, paid for by state or local authorities. Vouchers, of course, have been proposed by a wide variety of advocates as a means for introducing competition and accountability into the provision of public service, and some experiments with them have already been carried out and evaluated. To my knowledge, however, this is the first suggestion to use vouchers for the purpose of choosing and funding interest representatives—something that fits nicely with my general objective of making the experience of Euro-democracy different from its national counterpart without, of course, diminishing or damaging the latter.

The system I am proposing here would deliberately avoid the specification by European authorities of any fixed category of representation based on class, status, sector, profession, or cause but would leave the task of determining the organizational boundaries surrounding these entities to the initiative of interest entrepreneurs, the self-determination of social groups, and the subsequent competition for vouchers from individual citizens. The central purpose behind the development of such a semipublic status for Euro-associations and movements is to encourage them both to become better citizens (i.e., to treat each other on the basis of greater equality and mutual respect) and to dedicate greater attention to the interests and passions of the European public as a whole (i.e., to articulate those issues that transcend national boundaries).

This effort would involve nothing less that an attempt to establish a "Charter of Rights and Obligations" for European associations and movements that would, thereby, be recognized as "secondary (organizational) citizens of Europe"—alongside the usual individual variety that we have discussed earlier. It would be naive to suppose that merely imposing certain forms and rules would *eo ipso* make them into more "fact-regarding, other-regarding, and future-regarding" actors.[14] The legislation of most national democracies is strewn with unsuccessful attempts to regulate lobbies and pressure groups. What is distinctive about this approach is the coupling of respect for certain conditions of self-organization and management with quite concrete incentives for support and a competitive process of allocation.

It would be presumptuous of me to specify here all the rights and obligations that might be included in such a charter. This would require a great deal of comparative research into existing national legislation, for much of what would be involved is probably already on the books in one way or another in each of the member states. The purpose served by bringing it together in one formalized "Euro-status" and asking individual interest associations whether they would agree to abide by that specific package of rights and obligations would be to clarify ambiguities and jurisdictions—and to place eventual enforcement under a common source of authority (i.e., the ECJ).

For purposes of illustration only, I could imagine the following general provisions:

1. A special registration procedure and title for all associations operating under the charter that engage in the activity of interest representation/intermediation
2. A certification that it has members and some organizational presence in a minimum number of member states of the EU
3. An assurance of access to public authorities concerning all deliberations relevant to legislation and implementation in their respective interest domains (*Vernehmlassungsverfahren* is the inimitable Swiss German expression)
4. A guarantee of democratic procedures for the election of all executive officers and their accountability to the full membership, with provisions for the protection of minority rights
5. A commitment to accepting as members all individuals, firms, families, and so forth, whose interests fall within the association's self-defined domain of representation (i.e., without regard for partisan affiliation, gender, race, nationality, etc.)
6. A prohibition against the advocacy of violence, racism, and other forms of criminal behavior
7. A commitment to full public disclosure of associational revenues and expenditures
8. A prohibition against engaging in profit-making activities
9. A prohibition against contributing to the financing of political parties, social movements, or other interest associations (except those that are their members)

10. An assurance of their capacity to participate directly in the implementation of public policies—even a presumption that relevant
policies will be administered to the maximum feasible extent
through associational channels
11. A guarantee that public authorities will not intervene in the internal
deliberations and choices of semipublic associations, except to ensure compliance with the preceding provisions of their status and
the applicable sections of the civil and criminal codes
12. Finally, permission to receive public funds, raised by obligatory
contributions from citizens and distributed by EU voucher, in addition to funds raised voluntarily from members

In my opinion, this list does not represent a massive set of new entitlements or constraints. It more closely resembles a formalization and con-
densation of existing norms contained either in national legislation or in the
private constitutions of most interest associations and social movements—
with, however, their transposition to the level of the EU as a whole. In
other words, it is analogous to the effort that has been made (so far, unsuccessfully) to establish a uniform status for European business firms.

Obligatory Contributions

No one advocates the creation of a new tax lightly—especially these days
in the face of neoliberal diatribes against fiscal obligations that are supposed to be already too high. But this proposal rests squarely on the need
to develop a new method for financing interest intermediation that is independent of the ability and willingness of individual citizens to pay—and
that means extracting resources involuntarily from all those who ulti-
mately will benefit. It may be disguised under some innocuous label—for
example, "the Euro-representation Contribution"—but it would still have
to be a coercive levy.[15]

The contribution/tax should be extracted from all persons resident in a
given territory, but not from firms or corporations since they would be
forced to pay twice and could, therefore, exert more influence over the re-
sultant distribution of revenues (and would, in any case, just pass on the
cost to their consumers). Persons who wished could also give voluntarily
to various national and European causes, but this would not exempt them
from the general "representative contribution." Note that, by tolerating
such a freedom, small and compact "privileged groups" would still be
more likely to attract and spend disproportionate resources in the European policy process, since their members would continue to have greater
incentives to give voluntarily above and beyond their involuntary contribution. Nevertheless, given the large numbers involved across Europe as

a whole, a very considerable evening-out of resources across interest categories and passionate causes would be likely.

The most feasible manner for doing this would be to attach the proposed voucher system to the election of Euro-deputies. Even if the amounts involved are quite small, it will not be difficult to generate rather considerable sums. For example, if each Euro-citizen would be required to contribute the equivalent of a modest ten euros, that would raise the tidy sum of 2.81 billion euros in the EU (15) of today. That could fund a lot of associative action, and, depending on how citizens "spend" their vouchers, it could go a long way to rectifying existing inequities in organizational resources and systemic underrepresentation within Euro-institutions. What is important is to retain the low level of individual payments in order not to scare away potential supporters of the reform, but to make the aggregate level of resources provided sufficient to compensate for persistent inequalities between interests. It is also essential to convince the public that such an arrangement would constitute an important extension of democratic rights—analogous to the previous extension of the franchise. This is where the voucher notion comes in.

Citizen Vouchers

What pulls the entire scheme together is the mechanism of vouchers. These specially designated, nontransferable units of account could only be assigned to European-level interest associations with a semipublic status, in proportions chosen by the individual Euro-citizen. Their value would be established by the EP at some uniform level, and there would be no way of avoiding paying for them. The only cost involved in spending them would be the individual's time and effort in getting acquainted with alternative recipients, plus the few moments it would take to check off boxes or fill in blanks.

There are many attractive features of vouchers in the domain of specialized representation:

1. They would permit a relatively free expression of the multiplicity of each Euro-citizen's preferences, rather than confine them to one party list or a single candidate as do most territorially based voting systems.
2. They allow for an easy resolution of the "intensity problem" that has long plagued democratic theory, since their proportional distribution by individuals across associations should reflect how strongly the citizenry "really" feels about various interests and passions.[16]
3. They equalize the amount and sever the decision to contribute from the disparate command over resources that individual citizens un-

avoidably have in an economic system based on the unequal distribution of private property.

4. They offer no rational motive for waste or corruption since they cannot provide a direct or tangible benefit to the donor and can only be spent by certified associations for designated public purposes with the EU.

5. In fact, they should provide a very important incentive for reflection on the nature of one's interests, thereby encouraging the opening up of a new public space at the level of Europe as a whole. Since they would be repeated over time, the distribution of these vouchers would present a virtually unique opportunity to evaluate the consequences of one's past choices.

6. They would, therefore, become a powerful mechanism for enforcing the accountability of existing Euro-associations and movements since, if the behavior of their leaders differs too remarkably from the preferences of those who spent their vouchers on them, citizens could presumably transfer their vouchers elsewhere.

7. They make it relatively easy not just to switch among existing rival conceptions of one's interest but also to bring into existence previously latent groups that presently cannot make it over the initial organizational threshold.

8. Finally, they offer a means of extending the principle of Euro-citizenship and the competitive core of Euro-democracy[17] that neither makes immediate and strong demands on individuals nor directly threatens the entrenched position of elites.

Granted that in the initial iterations of the scheme, existing Euro-associations and movements that accepted semipublic status would naturally be at an advantage, although less so than the national ones whose names and symbols are better known and whose members are less likely to defect from the group loyalties they have already acquired. On the one hand, this could be thought of as desirable since it should lead these established Euro-level organizations to support the scheme in the first place. On the other hand, it might initially have the undesirable effect of perpetuating organizations that are no longer representative. Eventually, the logic of competitive appeals for vouchers should have the effect of either revivifying moribund groups or displacing them by more authentic rivals.

SEMICONCLUSIONS WITH REGARD TO REPRESENTATION

The problem with democratizing the Euro-polity's system of representation is not to create something ex novo, as was the case with Euro-citizenship. Plenty of interests and passions have already found their way to the corridors of Brussels. It is just that they are too skewed in functional terms toward business interests and too confined in territorial terms to groups articulated at the national level. Ironically, it may prove more difficult to improve this evolving system with its entrenched modes of access than to convince individual Europeans that the emerging Euro-polity can make a positive contribution to extending and guaranteeing their rights as citizens. Nevertheless, the potentiality for mobilizing the interests of other classes, sectors, and professions at the supra- and subnational levels—not to mention for reaching the passions behind so many social movements and environmental causes—exists, and, if realized, it could provide a new momentum to the whole integration process. The modest proposals for reform suggested in this chapter will definitely not eliminate the favored treatment of national and business interests (if they did, these proposals would no doubt be rejected *sine die*), but they should encourage the opening of new channels of representation and the experimenting with new means for holding authorities accountable. In the absence of a large-scale refounding (i.e., constitutionalizing, of the entire enterprise), I doubt whether one could ask anything more at this stage. And who knows—once some groups have demonstrated their success in representing "other" interests and passions, this could even trigger more generalized (and irrepressible) responses.[18] Whether this sort of politicization would—on balance—prove to be positive for European integration in the future is a calculated risk, but one that should be taken. Without such an effort at enlarging the sphere of representation and without much further prospect for cultivating functional spillovers surreptitiously, those who favor such an enterprise could, at best, find themselves defending a stagnant process and, at worse, managing a retreat to the *status quo ante integratio.*

AN EXCURSUS ON WHAT AN EVENTUAL
EURO-PARTY SYSTEM MIGHT LOOK LIKE

Stein Rokkan in a seminal article once analyzed the emerging party systems of Europe by juxtaposing the generic cleavage structures of each national society with its geopolitical location on the continent.[19] While he, self-admittedly, had the advantage of hindsight (i.e., he knew what configurations had emerged prior to World War I and hence could retrospectively trace their emergence backwards in time), it might be interesting to use some of the same assumptions and variables to reflect *prospectively* on what sort of party system could eventually assert itself at the level of the European Union.

For, *grosso modo*, the EU is presently in a situation roughly analogous with the national polities of its member states in the mid-1800s. Something like a party system already exists exclusively within the European Parliament and is used to structure its internal processes, but these cleavages and alliances do not yet extend to the embryonic Euro-citizenry in the form of stable identifications, shared symbols, and common platforms. The Euro-citizens have been voting directly since 1985 for supranational representatives, but they have been oriented primarily by national identifications, symbols, and platforms. Moreover, since the general perception is that these Euro-elections "do not count," these linkages have been "opportunistic" and have produced results that are typically more polarized than in national elections—either because only the zealously motivated have bothered to vote (and even then in decreasing numbers) or because moderate voters have used these elections to send a message of dissatisfaction back to their national politicians by choosing "fringe candidates" that they would never have supported in their more "meaningful" national or subnational elections.

What is more, Rokkan's second major hypothesis might just be proven by the EU experience. He observes that, once national party systems had emerged around a pattern of initial societal cleavages and geopolitical locations, they tended to "freeze" the subsequent identities and behaviors of citizens, even when the founding interests and passions declined in salience and other conflicts became stronger. If we could successfully capture the factors that are going to condition the emergence of such a supranational party system, then we have some reason to suspect that this configuration will endure for some time and hence continue to play a major role in consolidating whatever type of democracy will be formed. All this, of course, presumes something that is not yet apparent—namely, that the cleavages behind a Euro-party system have some degree of autonomy from those that are embedded in the experiences of its member states. If, as so far seems to be the case, the organizations that call themselves European parties are merely loose confederations adopting a least-common-denominator program and possessing virtually no organizational distinctiveness, then our exercise in speculation will have proven irrelevant.

FOCUSING ON EUROPEAN SOCIETAL CLEAVAGES

It is difficult to know what to make of Rokkan's geopolitical distinctions, since the present EU encompasses almost all of them. It has a "core area" consisting of the ancient city belt that extended from London to Florence with its Rhineland corridor, various economic and cultural peripheries with their distinctive languages and/or systems of production, differing legacies of colonialism and empire, land-locked and maritime-oriented units, and even an extensive (if yet to be defined) set of "marches" to the east. From a Rokkanian point of view, one can begin with the proposition that this heterogeneity in basic historical structures is a major obstacle to the formation of a viable Europe-wide party system—just as it was on a lesser scale in those national states such as France, Spain, Germany, Switzerland, and Italy that also were composed of distinctive, even previously independent, regions. These countries, however, had the "advantage" of having at their disposition the periodic use of coercion, either to suppress internal dissidence or to prosecute external war. Waging war and keeping the peace not only helped to produce a more unified sense of national identity but also contributed to nationalizing the party system. One can scarcely imagine the EU doing either, although the recent experience of participating in a common armed struggle against Yugoslavia/Serbia might just contribute something to overcoming mutual suspicions and instilling a sense of shared fate that did not exist before. The additional (and completely unprecedented) fact that the governments of the major protagonists (except for the United States) were all composed of politicians nominally linked to the same European Socialist Party may also be of some future importance.

In Rokkan's original model, these differences in historical points of departure for the national state-building experience interact in a variety of ways with the main axes of internal societal cleavage. These cleavages can still be found (to differing degrees) in most European states: (1) *class conflict* between capital and labor; (2) *regional competition* between center and periphery; (3) *sectoral clashes* between agriculture, industry and services; and (4) *religious struggles* between Catholics and Protestants. Were he alive, Rokkan would certainly acknowledge that their contemporary salience is not what it was during the heroic founding epoch of the late 1800s and early 1900s—which implies that were these countries to create ex novo their party systems today, they would come out with very different configurations. This, I suspect, holds even more for the EU.

Religious disputes between Catholics and Protestants have lost much of their intensity and capacity for citizen mobilization—either as the result of a general process of secularization or as a product of ecumenical convergence.[20] Their orientation has, moreover, shifted to the contrast between "European-Christian" denominations versus "non-European" ones, with various forms of Eastern Orthodoxy occupying an uneasy position in between. Some of the statements made (especially by Christian Democrats) in relation to eventual Turkish membership reflect this cleavage. Even more salient, however, has been the resistance within some member states to the growing numbers of Islamic immigrants in Europe and the role played by Islamic political militants. "Nativists" in these national contexts have tended to identify European integration as a key factor restricting their respective countries from following exclusionary policies, and, to the extent that they manage to mobilize across national borders, they could provide a solid basis for an extreme right-wing and militantly anti-EU party. At present, they are significantly underrepresented in the European Parliament (as are all anti-EU forces), but their numbers are growing and they could very well form an alliance with dissatisfied groups generated by other societal cleavages.

One of these, ironically, might be agriculture. Despite being one of the groups that has benefited directly the most from EU policies, they have to be numbered among the EU's firmest opponents. Since farmers are no longer numerous enough (at least, in the present fifteen member states) to establish their own party and since the historical opportunity to form a "Red-Green" alliance with urban working-class-based parties does not seem available, they might just be tempted to enter into a broader coalition of "integration losers"—provided that its leaders can come up with an ideology that is not too manifestly "fascist" and does not exacerbate nationalist tensions between member states.

Other sectoral clashes seem either very diffuse or fragmented into so many cross-cutting systems of production that they fail to produce the classic "we-they" pattern that seems so central to the dialectics of party formation and reproduction. One could imagine, however, some relatively stable interest coalitions between the more dynamic industries and services, on the one side, and the more traditional ones they are progressively displacing, on the other, but this is more likely to take the form of momentary campaigns over specific issues involving sectoral associations and subnational regions than to provide a stable basis for partisan identification.

Center-periphery remains a significant line of cleavage within and across European states. Even a brief glance at the territorial distribution of results in the referenda that were held at the time of the ratification of the Maastricht Treaty would reveal common patterns of pro-European support in the core areas and anti-European resistance in the peripheries. Of course, some former national peripheries, such as Flanders, Catalunya, Languedoc, the Alto Adige, and Voralberg, have become increasingly part of the core, thanks to their strategic location in the integration process. Some of these have even entered into so-called *Euro-regios* that cross national borders and seek to exploit their special status in order to attract industries and services for the emerging market. Presumably, with eventual enlargement to the east, some of Europe's most locationally disadvantaged areas are going to find themselves in the midst of new exchanges. So, "peripheral peripheries" will continue to be a problem and they too may join a mega-alliance of losers, but the sheer economic dynamism of the integration process itself, coupled with periodic incorporation of new members, will be constantly shifting the basis of the calculation.

Class conflict in its classical left-right configuration is still the mainstay of most national party systems, but its intensity has declined considerably. Not only has "class voting" diminished everywhere, but also parties have tended to be less and less preoccupied with attracting their historical core voters (*Stamwähler*) and more and more oriented to catching the shifting voters in the middle. Centripetal competition has replaced centrifugal competition—with the result that party platforms are increasingly hard to distinguish from each other. And their policies once in office are only marginally different.

Speculating about the Implications

From this sketch based on variations in Rokkan's original analysis, I come to the following speculative observations:

1. The cleavage patterns in Europe are even more multiple than was historically the case at the national level; hence, the emerging European party system will be less uniform, and, even when the politicians do manage to adopt the same symbols and programs across all member states, the parties running on this common basis will be much more fragmented into factions and less capable of exerting party discipline, either in parliament or in the nomination process.
2. The cleavages may be more multiple, but they are a lot less salient and capable of inspiring polarized attraction and repulsion. Hence, Euro-parties will be even more "centripetal" in their competition with each other (and bland in their respective platforms) than their national counterparts, many of whom are still living off a past political capital of strong antagonism.
3. Class conflict will continue to provide the major cleavage to the emerging Euro-party system, but it will be profoundly crosscut by

alliances along sectoral and center-periphery lines. Left and right will persist as general orienting labels, but as we have already seen at the national (and, very lately and embryonically, at the supranational) level, it will be preceded by various modifiers designed to appeal to the vast public in the middle.

4. New cleavages that were not envisaged by Rokkan may prove more salient in the emerging Euro-polity, even if they will tend to align themselves with the basic underlying left-right continuum. Many of these are rooting in generational conflicts, exacerbated by an aging population that is reserving an increasing proportion of total resources to itself and a young population that is bound to find less attractive job prospects than their elders. To the extent that many environmental issues are also "age graded," they will reinforce the tendency toward generation-based cleavages.

5. I suspect that what will emerge in the near future is a "2+2" party system in which two pro-European parties (one on the left and the other on the right) will compete for most of the votes and collude in the management of EU affairs—as they now do in the internal politics of the European Parliament. Anti-European parties will gradually increase in popular appeal (especially if little or nothing is done to democratize EU institutions), but they will be initially divided along left-right lines. What is not yet clear is whether these parties will compete for Euro-votes and Euro-seats in the EP or whether they will increasingly resort to "extraparliamentary" tactics to express their resistance to further integration.

6. If the "anti-Europeans" do choose to play according to EU rules in order to oppose it from within and if the left-right cleavage continues to decline in salience, then the longer-run prospect will be for the emergence of a two-party system in which two very heterogeneous coalitions (one pro and the other anti) will dominate—an outcome that superficially resembles the U.S. party system even if the central issue will be "state's rights" rather than social class.

The underlying message of all this should be rather obvious. If Euro-elections continue to be held regularly (and abolishing them would be very difficult), they will tend to produce results that will be increasingly at odds with the distribution of preferences registered in national and subnational elections. The emerging Euro-party system will be significantly different from the national ones: more fragmented and less disciplined; more centripetal for most voters but with centrifugal minorities increasing their strength on the extreme left and right; more open to the expression of new interests and causes, but less capable of breaking into the cartel of dominant parties.

Most problematically, unless major institutional reforms are introduced, these elections will attract an increasingly "unrepresentative sample" of citizens. With the monotonic decline in turnout already observed in each successive Euro-election, those who bother to vote will be ever more purposively (not randomly) distributed. The moderates will be less and less likely to take the trouble (and those who do so out of habit will be more aged) on the grounds that the EP has little or no relation to government or accountability; the extremes will see this more and more as an opportunity to get into the political game and to embarrass national governments at low cost without bearing any responsibility for their actions.

My hunch is that should this scenario materialize and national governing parties and coalitions be repeatedly and overtly disavowed by their respective Euro-electorates, the pressure could become so intense that these politicians might be tempted to introduce democratic reforms, if only to convince ordinary voters that Euro-elections are worth the effort. So far, it is these very same parties and coalitions that have been most wary about establishing a competing supranational representative assembly that would not only diminish the role of the Council of Ministers but might even undermine that of national parliaments. If, however, it is precisely the meaninglessness of Euro-elections that is having the indirect (and unintended) effect of calling the legitimacy of national politicians into question every five years, then they may decide to change their minds — and to take Euro-democracy seriously.

NOTES

1. My hunch is that, even in an orthodox federation—national or supranational—this may no longer be an adequate view of the process of democratic representation. It ignores the very substantial changes that have already taken place in the nature and role of parties in well-established democracies, and it anachronistically presumes that parties in today's emerging Euro-polity will go through all the developmental stages and perform all the functions of their national predecessors. It seems preferable (to me) to assume that the citizens of contemporary Europe have quite different organizational skills, are less likely to identify so closely with partisan symbols or ideologies, and are inclined to defend a much more variegated set of interests. Moreover, the Euro-polity is emerging in an international environment virtually saturated with different models of successful collective action. All this may not preclude a hegemonic role for political parties in the representation of social groups, but it does suggest that they will be facing more competition from interest associations and social movements than their predecessors and that we should revise our thinking about democratization accordingly.

2. Another way of putting the issue is that, while future European integration will have to give up the presumption of a uniformly expanding *acquis communautaire* for all members in all policy arenas, it should be possible to safeguard a core subset of mutual obligations sufficient to prevent excessive "free riding" and "predation."

3. According to my understanding, this has long been the practice in the Italian parliament—perhaps, not a model of legislative probity, but a formidable producer of laws. Giuseppe Di Palma, *Surviving without Governing* (Berkeley: University of California Press, 1977).

4. The European Parliament already has a "bureau" composed of its president and fourteen vice presidents, all elected by the plenum.

5. The fact that Euro-deputies are elected according to rather disparate electoral regimes is, no doubt, regrettable from a strictly democratic point of view, but it is not clear whether this has significant consequences for the way in which they "process" the demands of their constituents. For a comprehensive discussion of the different regimes, see Julián Santamaría, Josep María Renid, and Vicente Cobos, "Los debates sobre el procedimiento electoral uniforme y las carateristicas diferenciales de las elecciones europeas," *Revista de estudios politicos* 90 (October–December 1995): 11–44.

6. What might not be so difficult to implement would be the provision of funds to MEPs for the purpose of holding hearings or *assises* in their respective districts once they have been elected. One of the major problems of EU representation—namely, the physical and psychological distance from constituencies to the institutions in Brussels and Strasbourg—might be mitigated by such an investment.

7. *Flexible Integration: Towards a More Effective and Democratic Europe* (London: Centre for European Policy Research, 1995), 172.

8. The best and most up-to-date treatment I have read on this subject is Frank L. Wilson, "The Elusive European Party System," paper presented at the ECSA

meeting, Charleston, S.C., May 11–14, 1995. For an earlier analysis, see Karl-Heinz Reif and Oskar Niedermayer, "The European Parliament and the Political Parties," *Journal of European Integration* 10, nos. 2 and 3 (1987): 157–72.

9. For example, it might be desirable to "relax" the seven-hundred-seat rule for the European Parliament and offer an additional twenty-five or so seats to MEPs elected from transitional districts over a certain size (say, two hundred thousand citizens). Some of the existing Euro-regios are that large and include as many as four member states. Needless to say, citizens from these districts would not be allowed to vote twice but would have to choose whether they preferred to be represented in transnational or subnational constituencies.

10. One desirable innovation might be to condition the amount of the subsidy for conducting EU elections upon absolute turnout in the previous EU election. Countries that managed to encourage more of their Euro-citizens to vote would be rewarded with greater funds; those that suffered greater abstention would be (modestly) punished. As it presently stands, there is no reward for better performance (just as there are no controls on how money is spent), and one could even suspect that by not running an aggressive and expensive campaign, national parties indirectly promote abstention—and reward themselves by banking the surplus to be used in contests that they consider more important.

11. *The Semi-Sovereign People* (Hinsdale, Ill.: Dryden, 1975), originally published in 1960.

12. Wolfgang Streeck and Philippe C. Schmitter, "From National Corporatism to Transnational Pluralism: Organized Interests in the Single European Market," *Politics & Society* 19, no. 2 (June 1991): 133–64; also Franz Traxler and Philippe C. Schmitter, "The Emerging Euro-Polity and Organized Interests," *European Journal of International Relations* 1, no. 2 (June 1995): 191–218.

13. "Interests, Associations and Intermediation in a Reformed Post-Liberal Democracy," *Politische Vierteljahresschrift* 35, Sonderheft 25, "Staat und Verbaende" (1994): 160–74.

14. For this "trilogy" of types of regardingness, I am indebted to Claus Offe.

15. The tax would be novel, but the amounts of revenue transferred to interest associations might not be. Since first presenting this idea in Norway several years ago, I have become increasingly aware of the very substantial sums that some continental European governments provide as subsidies to specific organizations—ostensibly because they are accomplishing some public purpose. Norway, Spain, and France are three cases in point, even if the amounts involved are rarely publicized.

At the level of the EU, no one knows for sure how much funding is presently devoted to the purpose of supporting Euro-associations, although they have been so substantial that the EP has periodically demanded an investigation of them. This subsidization of civil society by bureaucratic means is much less democratic than the one that I propose since the criteria used to determine eligibility are secret and noncompetitive, whereas under a voucher-based scheme, this would all take place publicly and accountably and would be accompanied by specific binding obligations to behave as "secondary citizens." If the countries (and the European Union) that are presently subsidizing associations by clandestine means would agree to stop these practices, they might be able to switch to a better arrangement at virtually no cost!

16. Not incidentally, they also would generate a fabulous new source of data on preferences for social scientists to analyze—much cheaper and much better in quality than what they have been collecting via survey research.

17. See my earlier essay, "Democratic Theory and Neo-Corporatist Practice," *Social Research* 50, no. 4 (Winter 1983): 885–928, in which I evaluate the role of competitiveness along with such other normative standards for democracy as participation, access, responsiveness, and accountability.

18. There are already some signs of this, especially coming from the pressure of environmental movements. The EP has recently rejected several directives coming from the commission. For a case study of one such "footnote," see David Earnshaw and David Judge, "The European Parliament and the Sweeteners Directive: From Footnote to Inter-Institutional Conflict," *Journal of Common Market Studies* 31, no. 1 (March 1993): 103–16.

19. "Nation-Building, Cleavage Formation and the Structuring of Mass Politics," in S. Rokkan, *Citizens Election Parties* (Oslo: Universitetsforlaget, 1970), 72–144; also Seymour Martin Lipset and Stein Rokkan, "Cleavage Structures, Party Systems and Voter Alignments: an Introduction," in *Party Systems and Voter Alignments,* ed. S. M. Lipset and S. Rokkan (New York: Free Press, 1967), 1–64.

20. It has been the source of some controversy the fact that all but one of the politicians who played a founding role in the original EEC were public representatives of Catholic parties. Since then, Christian or Christian Democratic parties have been the most consistent supporters of the integration process, whether at the national or the supranational level. Protestant parties (where they exist) and Protestant countries (most prominently in the north of Europe) have been markedly more reluctant to join the EC/EEC/EU or to accept enhanced powers for its institutions. Gary Marks and Carole J. Wilson have suggested that this may be due to differences in their ecclesiastical structure: the Roman Catholic Church is already a supranational organization; virtually all of the Protestant denominations are national. "The Past in the Present: A Cleavage Theory of Party Response to European Integration," unpublished paper, University of North Carolina at Chapel Hill, no date, 10–11. This historical cleavage may persist within the member countries (and there are abundant signs that it is declining), but I find it implausible that it will be replicated at the level of Europe as a whole.

4

Decision Making

The European Union may lack an explicit constitution, but it has plenty of rules that prescribe how its decisions should be made and how its institutions should relate to each other when making those decisions. Moreover, these rules and relations seem to be regularly followed, even if there can be considerable ambiguity about how they are meant to apply in specific cases.[1] While it is frequently claimed that the EU decision making is slow, inefficient, secretive, biased, technocratic, and certainly not democratic, the "system" is not manifestly in crisis—although further enlargement, especially to the east, raises the prospect that it might simply collapse as a consequence of the sheer increase in the number of member states and the greater heterogeneity of their interests.[2]

For it is certainly arguable that *the EU is already the most complex polity that human agency*—in this case acting through successive negotiations between member states—*has ever devised.* And even then, not all of its rules and practices have been formerly approved or explicitly stated. Whole institutions or "arrangements" of major importance have barely been acknowledged to exist.[3] Nevertheless, it is possible to get a reasonably accurate picture of how the EU works by studying the detailed provisions of its multiple treaties, supplemented by the joint declarations periodically announced by heads of state and government at the meetings of the European Council and the clarifying decisions made episodically by the European Court of Justice. By comparison, the rules and structures of any existing national state—even the most federalized or decentralized—would look like models of rationality and simplicity.

The European Parliament can claim the dubious distinction of having twenty formally different decision-making procedures.[4] The Council of Ministers is supposedly composed of three distinct "pillars," and the rules are formally different in each of them. Even within the first pillar, that of economic liberalization and market regulation, some decisions can be taken by simple majority, others by qualified majority, and still others by unanimity. A good deal of the power of the commission presumably rests formally on its monopoly over the introduction of all new decisions, regulations, and directives—each of which, incidentally, takes a different decisional trajectory—but informally this rule has been increasingly "bent" by initiatives coming from the European Council and the European Parliament, as well as from various national governments working behind the scenes.[5]

THE CAPACIOUS NATURE OF DEMOCRATIC RULES

As we have seen in the first chapter, competition and cooperation among representatives are essential for ensuring the accountability of rulers to the citizenry in all forms of modern democracy. However, the rules and relations that are supposed to channel these processes of competition and cooperation have been quite varied across historical time and geocultural space. Our democratic ancestors in classical Greece relied heavily on selection by lot to fill positions of authority and presumed that most decisions would be taken by consensus. The citizenry was expected to agree unanimously or at least overwhelmingly after listening to debates about the merits and demerits of alternative courses of action. Those who persistently disagreed did so at their peril and were sometimes forced into exile or, as in the case of Socrates, death.

This classical democratic tradition of hostility to "faction," "adversarial behavior," "special interests," and "partial wills" persists in the more utopian versions of what the practice of democracy should be, but at least since the *Federalist Papers* in the 1780s it has become widely accepted that competition and cooperation among representatives of persistent factions are "necessary evils" in all democracies that operate at a more than local scale with a less than homogenous population. Hence, selection of officials by lot and decisions based on the presumption of unanimity or consensus have been replaced by more explicit procedures of nomination and election and by more elaborate rules for determining who among contending candidates should be elected and which among contending projects should become binding upon all. What remains "essentially contested," however, are what these democratic procedures and rules should be in a particular political context.

Granted, there is a widely diffused and commonly accepted image of democracy that identifies it exclusively with *rule by the majority*. Accordingly, any governing body that makes decisions by combining the votes of more than half of those present and eligible to vote is said to have acted democratically—whether that majority emerges from an electorate, a parliament, a committee, a city council, or a party caucus. For specific occasions—say, the amendment of a constitution or the expulsion of a member—the rule is often bent, and "qualified majorities" of more than 51 percent or "weighted majorities" that give specific groups or persons more votes than others may be required.

What is incontestable is that modern democracy involves some process of assembling representatives (and, occasionally, citizens in referenda or town meetings) and counting their preferences in some way so that a legitimate decision binding upon all can be taken. The problem of how to do this arises when *numbers* collide with *intensities*—when a perfectly properly assembled and accurately counted majority (especially if it is a stable majority across many issues) produces decisions that negatively affect some minority (especially if that minority is a stable cultural, ethnic, or national group that feels intensely threatened). In these circumstances, where some element of social or cultural diversity intervenes to call into question the very existence of a single *demos* with relatively equal preferences and intensities, the practice of successful democracies has been to displace, if not replace, the majority principle with some other decision rule that recognizes disproportionately or protects explicitly the preferences of minority *demoi* within the same political process.

This can and has been accomplished in several ways. Constitutional provisions can place certain matters in "Bills of Rights" that are permanently beyond the reach of majorities. Territorial authorities in specified local or regional units can be guaranteed autonomous powers over issues of special concern to their subnational citizens. Representatives can be required to produce majorities on repeated occasions or across different constituencies. Votes can be weighted by complex formulae to compensate for such persistent deficiencies as small size, peripheral location, prior discriminatory treatment, or inferior level of development. On a more episodic and temporary basis, democracies have been governed by "grand coalitions" that incorporate almost all parties, and/or they have negotiated "social partnerships" that involve the participation of a broad spectrum of contending class, sectoral and professional interests.

Different mixes of these policies for dealing with numbers and intensities can produce different types of democracy. In Figure 4.1, I have proposed a means for defining these types that is neither dependent on formal institutional criteria nor restricted to the public, territorial, and electoral aspect of politics. Admittedly, the scheme is rather abstract and specifies not so much a limited number of nominal or ordinal types as an extensive property space within which individual cases—including that of the EU—can be plotted.[6]

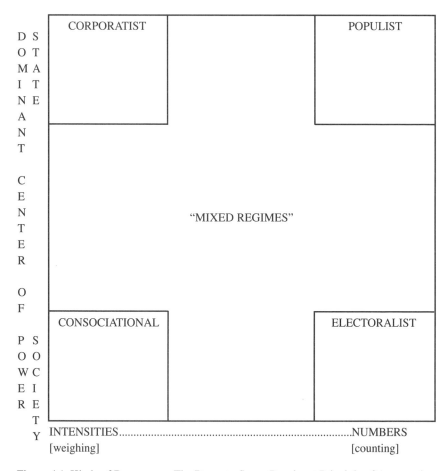

Figure 4.1 Kinds of Democracy: The Property Space Dominant Principle of Aggregation

The horizontal axis is defined in terms of what we have been discussing—that is, what decision rule is *the dominant principle of aggregation*. Is the democracy organized predominantly according to the principle of counting equally the sheer number of its citizens that support a given candidacy or policy? Or is it ordered in such a way that it tends to weigh the intensity of its citizen's preferences, whether aggregated according to class, religion, region, *ethnies,* or nationality? Both principles can claim validation in democratic theory, although they lead to quite different institutional expressions. This dimension captures in slightly altered language the basic underlying distinction stressed by Arend Lijphart.[7] At the one end are the majoritarian democracies in which decisions are made and justified in terms of the equal aggregation of preferences across the unit as a whole—broken down in some federalist cases by multiple levels of governance. At the other are those in which authoritative allocations depend on the formation of a much broader consensus by extensive deliberation and compromise among subunits of unequal size and intensities of preference.

The vertical axis picks up a second dimension of fundamental choice that affects all democracies operating in liberal-capitalist societies in which the distinction is drawn between a private domain of voluntary contracts and individual property rights and a public domain of involuntary control and collective political objectives. This *mix of public authority and private activity* has generated considerable controversy among proponents of democracy, beginning with the struggle between the Jacobins and the Girondins during the French Revolution over whether democracy is better served by an active and capable state that intervenes to rectify inequalities generated by other social and economic institutions and to ensure that the formal rights of citizenship can be exercised effectively, or whether democracy is better assured by relying on the competitive interactions between individuals and institutions in civil society and by restricting the role of the state to policing contracts made voluntarily and spontaneously by these private actors.

The former, "statist" conception of democracy may be presently on the ideological defensive, but it has by no means disappeared at either the subnational, national or supranational level of decision making. Severe economic depression, war, or even a significant increase in the level of international threat perception could bring it back very quickly. The latter, "societal," or just plain "liberal" conception of democracy has become virtually hegemonic in recent decades. The Single European Act, for example, seemed to have established a firm presumption in favor of private exchange over public authority in the operation of the EU, but the need to regulate those market processes to ensure fair and equal treatment among national producers—plus the subsequent increase in massive unemployment throughout the region—has brought about something of a revival of the notion that collective and coercive action at the supranational level might be necessary to fulfill citizen demands and popular expectations.

Please note that Figure 4.1 leaves lots of room for "impure" cases. Only the four extreme corners are given specific labels: corporatist, consociational, populist, and electoralist. The rest, especially the space located right in the middle of the figure, should be characterized as "mixed-type" democracies. The literature from Polybius through Montesquieu to the American founding fathers consistently stresses the desirable features of such mixed polities. It is arguable that the contrasting qualities of differ-

ent ruling formulas—concentrated and dispersed, territorial and functional, popular and elitist, accountable and autonomous, federal and unitary, compulsory and voluntary—can complement each other's virtues
and countermand each other's vices.

THE EU AS AN EMERGING
(IF STILL INCOMPLETE) TYPE OF DEMOCRACY

As we have seen in chapter 1, the EU can be classified—provisionally and
prospectively—far to the left in Figure 4.1. It is a rather extreme case of
a type of democracy that weighs intensities very carefully, especially
when those intensities are aggregated and expressed as "national interests." Only on the most trivial matters are numbers counted—and even
then, the numbers per national unit are weighed according to some (not always self-evident) formula of proportionality. Not only are small countries given a greater weight in the decision rules of the Council of Ministers, but unanimity is still required on a wide range of issues.[8] To a limited
extent, the codecision procedures introduced by the TEU resemble those
of a confederal system of concurrent majorities, while the fact that each
member country gets to nominate one or two commissioners and, therefore, all participate in a sort of "grand coalition" government bears a general similarity to a more consociational type of governance. The absence
(so far) of statutory guarantees for the separate powers of national and
supranational authorities—pace the frequent invocation of the principle of
subsidiarity—indicates that the Euro-polity is still far from the sort of federal "overlapping consensus" that might permit the development of more
numerical, majoritarian, decision rules.

The EU can also be safely placed—at least, for the immediate future—
toward the bottom of Figure 4.1. Voluntary exchanges between firms and
consumers, and voluntary agreements between units of civil society tend
to predominate over active interventions or coercive redistributions by
public authorities. For one thing, the EU's budget is far too small—and
member-state resistance to increasing it far too great—for it to play a serious statist role in competition with national states. The only exception is
the Common Agricultural Policy (CAP) through which it does redistribute serious amounts of money from European consumers to its farmers.
Repeated efforts by the commission (and, most recently, by its former
president, Jacques Delors) to create a viable "social dialogue" among organized capital, labor, and themselves have yet to succeed in channeling
the intensities of class-based interests in its direction. The more formal
Economic and Social Council has not made a serious contribution to
EEC/EC/EU decision making since its founding in the late 1950s. What

has made more of an impact are the large numbers of more specialized class, sectoral, and professional associations that have formed at the European level (often with the sponsorship of the commission). Especially since the signing of the Single European Act in 1985, Brussels has been literally invaded by "Euro-lobbies"—not just formal interest organizations but also a considerable variety of social movements, large enterprises, and law firms. While all this pluralism (to use the American expression) is entirely appropriate in a modern democracy, its highly skewed nature does raise some questions about whether these channels for the expression of particular intensities are freely and fairly available to all citizens of Europe. So far, the evidence suggests a mobilization of bias in favor of business interests.[9]

THE ROLE OF GENERAL PRINCIPLES

Before plunging into the heart of the matter (i.e., into relatively specific changes in decision rules that might be expected to improve the quality—and quantity—of Euro-democracy), let us first try to capture what is at stake in a more general fashion. Prospective democratizers of the EU must begin with member states that have rather entrenched national democratic institutions (whose politicians may not welcome being upstaged by competition for citizen attention coming from the supranational level), and they must deal with a less well-entrenched but nevertheless extremely complex European decision-making system that is already in place (whose politicians-cum-technocrats may not be disposed to open up their operations to greater transparency and accountability). If we combine these constraints with the observation made above that the present Europolity of fifteen is not (yet) in serious crisis, then there doesn't seem much likelihood that any significant reforms can be accomplished. Nevertheless, as we shall see in the excursus on agency in the next chapter, the prospect that the situation could get worse if the EU were more or less compelled to take on ten to thirteen new members and the reality that there are signs of growing dissent and disaffection among those who are already members do open up some possibility for more significant change than might otherwise be the case.

What is needed are some guidelines—based on principles that are popularly intelligible and politically defensible—that could guide that reform effort. Just tinkering with details in the name of greater efficiency (which accounts for the modest progress made via the Treaty of Amsterdam) is unlikely to produce much effect.

Simplification is one obvious candidate. The existing rules are virtually unintelligible even to experts, much less citizens. But this must be accomplished while respecting the diversity of situations in which national (and subnational) member states find themselves. Whatever changes are introduced, it should be stressed that any eventual Euro-democracy will be different (i.e., more remote, more indirect, more layered, more vicarious, and more complex) than the national democracies that compose it.

In the discussion of representation in chapter 3, we have already surreptitiously introduced to two potentially apposite principles: pertinence and proportionality.

Functional Pertinence

Representatives of national or subnational constituencies only have a right to participate with voice and vote in decisions made in those functional areas for which their governments have accepted full and identical commitments. The emerging Euro-polity seems condemned to having to tolerate "opt-outs" with regard to specific policies by standing members and may even later come to have to tolerate them for new members—provided that they are complete. There can be no question of joining "part" of monetary unification or "part" of a collective defense arrangement; the resulting decision-making problem would be unmanageable. And only if a given country accepts the full menu can it expect to participate legitimately in further policy making with regard to it. Even those who request temporary *dérogations* would not be entitled to vote until they had successfully met their deferred obligations (although they might be given a right to voice in the meantime).

Proportional Proportionality

The usual democratic principle of strict equality at the level of individual citizens would have to be waived in favor of a formula that explicitly recognized the unequal size of the historical units within which these citizens live and identify themselves. This diversity may have been historically accidental and unfortunate, but it is worth preserving, and the only way of doing so is to systematically overrepresent the citizens of small states and to protect them institutionally from being constantly outvoted by the citizens of large states. I propose to operationalize this principle by applying the square root value, rather than the absolute value, of a country's citizenry or population as the basis for allocating weighted votes in the Council of Ministers and seats in the European Parliament. If the larger countries refuse to recognize the wisdom of proportionate proportionality and insist on the application of strictly equal numerical decision-making rules, then, I submit, the effort to democratize the Euro-polity by voluntaristic and peaceful means is doomed to fail. The only alternative would be to create an imperial democracy, based on the assertion of hegemony by a single member state (read: Germany) or, more likely, a "directorate" of member states (read: a Franco-German axis).

The most neutral criterion on which to base proportionality would seem to be *size of the citizenry* of the preexisting national unit—rather than, say, level of development or geographic location. Virtually all Europeans recognize that they live in national societies of different sizes, that this is predictably connected with varying intensities of feeling with regard to language use, cultural preferences, institutional peculiarities, and so forth. Moreover, there is no overwhelming desire to eliminate this diversity. Indeed, the major problem in recent decades has been to contain it within existing national boundaries.

Not Quite So Modest Proposal 12

So, why not embed this recognizable and defensible diversity of size in the permanent decision-making structure of Euro-democracy by creating three (or more) *colegii based on the relative size of their respective citizenries*?

- One composed of the largest states with 60.4 to 39.0 million citizens (i.e., at the moment one composed of Germany, France, the United Kingdom, Italy, and Spain)
- A second composed of middle-size states with 11.6 to 6.3 million citizens: the Netherlands, Greece, Portugal, Belgium, and Sweden
- A third composed of small states with 5.4 to 0.2 million citizens: Austria, Finland, Denmark, Ireland, and Luxembourg

With enlargement, it should be possible to slot the new member states into one of these three clusters without diluting their significance, although something special might have to be done to accommodate such ministates as Andorra, Liechtenstein, San Marino, and Monaco if they should choose to join.[10]

Within each cluster, the number of deputies for the European Parliament and the number of weighted votes in the Council of Ministers (or eventual Upper House) would be disproportionate in absolute terms—roughly proportionate, as I have suggested, to the square root of the total size of their respective citizenries or populations. Hence, for example, if the European Parliament as a whole were to be limited to about seven hundred MEPs, that would presume about four hundred thousand citizens on the average for each deputy (with the present contingent of fifteen).[11] That could be fixed as the average for the middle *colegio*, but a higher average coefficient (say, five hundred thousand citizens per MEP) would be applied to the large *colegio* and a lower coefficient (say, two hundred thousand) to the small *colegio*.

An equivalent weighting of votes could be applied in the Council of Ministers, where it might be desirable to limit their total number to one hundred in order to facilitate calculation (and protect against the tendency for vote inflation in the future). As new members were admitted, the ratios would shift in order to remain within the overall limit of seven hundred seats in the EP and one hundred votes in the Council of Ministers.[12]

Not Quite So Modest Proposal 13

By far the most consequential and contentious matter that will have to be resolved if the Euro-polity is to be democratized will be the specific rules that permit either the European Council or the Parliament to take a decision that will be authoritatively binding, even on those members who disagree with it. Empowering EU institutions to override the unanimity rule, even for serious issues in pillars 2 and 3 (foreign affairs and internal security), would mean a definitive break with "intergovernmentalism" and is unlikely to be enacted without considerable resistance. No doubt, it will have to be introduced gradually, and, should either the *consortio* or *condominio* model prevail, individual countries would be protected by their opt-out option with regard to specific functional policy areas—provided, as I have argued earlier, they continue to respect the minimum, *noyau dur*, of common obligations.[13] Nevertheless, such an irreversible transformation is essential if the entire enterprise is to become credible as an efficient decision-making body that can move beyond the will of its least supportive member. It has already acquired this status through qualified majority voting on issues of the liberalization and regulation of its internal market and in its external trade negotiations with third parties. If the project of monetary unification moves ahead in the next years, the Euro-polity will have taken a further very substantial step in this direction—without, it should be noted, making any progress on democratization.

One principle that just might permit such an institutional breakthrough is that of *concurrent majorities* (CM). Instead of applying the standard principle of simple or qualified, one-time majorities for the approval of legislation, the future Euro-democracy could work on the basis of multiple, concurrent majorities.[14] The basic principle is simple: No measure would pass the Council of Ministers unless it obtained a majority in each of the three *colegii*—a simple majority for ordinary directives and perhaps a qualified majority for such matters as amendments to the rules or admission of new members.[15] This should be sufficient to reassure the smaller countries that they will not be outvoted *as a category* by the larger ones, although each country would still face the imperative of convincing a sufficient number of the fellow members of its *colegio* to reject a measure that it regarded as a specific threat to its national interests. The *liberum veto* or unanimity rule would disappear but be replaced by a "categoric" form of protection according to size.[16]

Needless to say, this reform would not do away with the possibility that lobbying and log rolling might take place across the three *colegii* on any given issue or issues, but that is not intrinsically undemocratic. Large countries might very well attempt to "bully" or "buy off" selected countries in the other two *colegii* to get what they want. In any case, the small and medium-size countries would be accorded a few more chips to bargain with than might otherwise be the case. Moreover, if the proposal to attach several referendum items to the usual Euro-elections were to prosper, the large countries would be periodically capable of demonstrating the existence of widespread support for specific measures—even if the results of these referenda were merely advisory.

Nota bene that the concurrent majority principle would itself run concurrently with the functional pertinence and proportionate proportionality principles. The requisite majorities would only have to be assembled among those member states that had accepted the full set of obligations in a given functional area, and the weighting of seats in the parliament or votes in the council would remain approximately proportionate to the value of the square root of the total size of the member state's citizenry.

Modest Proposal 14

The concurrent majority principle could also be applied to resolving the delicate problem of *the presidency of the Council of Ministers*. As it now stands, each member state occupies that office on a rotational basis for six months—which now means every 7.5 years. If and when membership expands to twenty-five or twenty-eight countries, the interval will become even more considerable. Since there is anecdotal (but convincing) evidence that this honor is especially great for small countries—imagine Lisbon, Ljubljana, and Luxembourg as the capital of Europe for successive six-month periods!—there are good reasons not to do away with this, despite its obvious inefficiency. One solution would be to establish a troika, not on the present basis of the past, present, and future presidencies but on the basis of the three *colegii*. Each presidency of the council would consist of three executives, one elected by each *colegio*, for a longer period of time—say, eighteen months or two years. Each *colegio* could work out its own rules for picking its representative, although collegiality itself would probably dictate some rotational formula. Nevertheless, the electoral format would allow for significant degrees of flexibility so that participation in the troika would not have to conflict with pressing national problems or momentary difficulties. Needless to say, the three executives would have to establish a division of labor among themselves, and it might prove prudent to have the representative from the large *colegio* take special responsibility for issues in the so-called second pillar of international security and foreign affairs, but that should be left to informal agreement, not written into formal statute.

Modest Proposal 15

The same general troika principle could be applied to the complex issue of *the nomination of commissioners, the choice of the president of the commission, and the distribution of portfolio responsibilities.* Whatever the number of commissioners, that should depend on the number of ministerial-level functional tasks to be filled—not, as is presently the case, on the larger countries nominating two and the smaller ones nominating a single commissioner. With enlargement, the number will easily exceed a manageable size for such a collegial body and become infested with national nominees who will have no real tasks to fulfill. An alternative worth considering would be to have them chosen by the three *colegii*, with each one proposing one-third of the total number of commissioners. The process of deliberation among one's peers may improve the quality of those nominated, and it is highly likely that some rotational calculations will prevail so that each country will have some chance of having its "own" commissioner over a foreseeable period of time—but not be guaranteed that it will always have one. This latter privilege is, to say the least, highly paradoxical under the present rules since each national commissioner is immediately required to swear that he or she will not take instructions from his or her government! It would be preferable to retain the broad representativeness of the commission in order to prevent the predominance of any one national administrative tradition, but to sever the connection with nomination by specific governments.

Modest Proposal 16

The president of the commission could be nominated for a fixed term by the troika then occupying the presidency of the European Council (needless to say, after extensive consultations with all of the member states) and would have to be approved by a majority of each of the *colegii* in the council (as well as by an absolute majority in the European Parliament), and the same decision rule would apply to the approval of his or her eventual choices to fill specific portfolios (of course, after all of the appropriate hearings had been conducted).[17] Subsequently, to improve accountability and to reinforce collegiality (as well as to reassure the smaller states), each of the commissioners would be personally responsible before the *colegio* that nominated him or her. Neither the large countries voting en bloc nor the parliament as a whole would be empowered to dismiss individually the nominees of smaller *colegii*, although as is presently the case the latter would collectively have the power to dismiss the commission as a whole.

It should be noted that these suggestions about decision-making rules within and between institutions of the Euro-polity do nothing to improve what has been, heretofore, one of the key weaknesses of Euro-democracy—namely, the absence of parties and a party system that operate credibly at the supranational level. Other than the modest reforms in the representation process designed to increase their role in Euro-elections through the nomination and financing of candidates that were proposed in chapter 3, I see no way to engineer an improvement of their role in the formation of the commission. Unless and until they develop a greater presence in the expectations of Euro-citizens, it would be simply artificial to assign them the usual key function that they perform in a parliamentary democracy (i.e., that of either forming or dissolving a government). The Euro-polity may well be headed in the general direction of parliamentarism, but its core constituencies will remain countries (and, perhaps, *colegii* of countries) for some time to come, not transnational political parties.[18]

THE EMBARRASSING SIDE ISSUE OF "GUARDIANSHIP"

Democratic theory does not like to admit it, but all existing democracies depend on the presence in their midst of nondemocratic institutions that deal with specific issues in confidential and authoritative ways that remove them from close scrutiny by representatives or the public as a whole. Robert Dahl has proposed the generic label, *guardianship*, to refer to this growing tendency.[19] The armed forces, intelligence services, and monetary authorities are among the most obvious examples, even if they may be held ex post accountable to standing parliamentary committees, special commissions of inquiry, or other forums of public disclosure. In modern welfare democracies, these technocratic bodies have tended to proliferate, often in the form of what are called in the United States "independent regulatory agencies."

The EU is no exception to this pattern. The agreed-on statutes of the eventual European Central Bank would endow it with a degree of political autonomy that even its *Vorbild*, the German Bundesbank, does not have. Various other specialized agencies for the recognition of patents, the protection of the environment, the approval of drugs, and so forth, have been set up or are in the process of being set up. It does not seem excessive to imagine that there will eventually be dozens of them—no doubt artfully distributed among the member states. And this does not include several intergovernmental organizations such as the Council of Europe (CoE), the United Nations Economic Commission for Europe (ECE), the Western European Union (WEU), or the Council on Security and Cooperation in Europe (CSCE) that maintain some "tangential" relation to the EU and overlap with its functions.

In its classic neofunctionalist strategy, European integration was supposed to develop, via successive spillovers, around a single bureaucratic-political center: the commission. To the extent that representatives of citizens would be able to influence the formation of that institution and subsequently control its decision making and policy implementation, then the whole emerging complex of supranational governance could (somehow) be described as democratic. But to the extent that the EU is drifting toward either *consortio* or *condominio* status under which each of these agencies would have its own autonomous governance structures and (perhaps) distinctive set of members, this presumption becomes less and less plausible. One could even imagine a scenario under which the key institutions of the present EU could be increasingly submitted to democratic accountability, while the actual functional substance of what is regulating the everyday life of European producers and consumers could be parceled out to these technocratic agencies—explicitly set up to be, not just "beyond the nation-state" but also "beyond the Euro-citizen."

It may seem premature even to be raising this issue, given the far more pressing ones of reforming the decision-making rules and relations of major EU institutions, and I must confess that I have few practical solutions to offer. The most obvious would be to establish permanent oversight functions for each specialized regulatory agency within the committee structure of the European Parliament. These sites—to which only those countries that accepted the pertinent *acquis* would have access— should also play an important role in approving appointments of Euro-agency executives, perhaps in response to candidates nominated by the council. Whatever the eventual format, it may well be worth while giving the issue of democratic control (and protection from "agency capture" by special interests) some thought *before* rather than *after* all these bodies are given their statutes, assigned their locations and begin their operations. For, if I am correct about the drift toward *consortio* or, even more, toward *condominio*, these emerging patterns of guardianship could represent a rather considerable future hazard for Euro-democratization.

SEMICONCLUSIONS ABOUT DECISION MAKING

There is no question that most of the political potential—both for improving the effectiveness of EU institutions and for democratizing them—
lies in reforming decision-making rules and relations of EU institutions.
The proposals for improving Euro-citizenship and Euro-representation
offer relatively less significant and, especially, less immediate payoffs. At
best, they might alter the expectations and practices of future generations.
Moreover, if implemented without any concomitant modifications in decision making, they would lose a good deal of their credibility. It is only
if citizens and representatives are sufficiently confident that the rules are
fair and responsive to their newly acquired identities and capabilities, that
they will be willing to invest more time and energy in them. And there is
no question that the present institutional arrangements offer only very limited incentives to most individuals and categories of interest.

The principles I have sought to operationalize—functional pertinence,
proportionate proportionality, voting by *colegii,* and concurrent majorities—are hardly the most common ones in the conceptual arsenal of
democracy. Indeed, all four "stretch" the usual principles as they apply to
relatively homogenous national states in order to fit them into the heterogeneous nonstate of the EU. This means that ordinary citizens and their
representative politicians may have some initial difficulty in recognizing
them as "really" democratic.

A great deal depends on whether relative size can serve as a generally
acceptable criteria for differentiation—and not level of development, cultural affinity, ideological orientation, or geographic location—and
whether it can produce clusters of countries whose citizens are capable of
identifying with each other. If so, then the question becomes whether the
formation of concurrent majorities across these clusters would be sufficient to satisfy the three contradictory imperatives of EU decision making: (1) to prevent a narrow minority of Euro-citizens aggregated in (overrepresented) small countries or (underrepresented) large countries from
blocking any decision from being made, (2) to prevent an artificial majority composed of (overrepresented) small countries from jamming
through decisions against the overwhelming majority of Euro-citizens living in (underrepresented) large countries, and (3) to prevent the formation
of a stable bloc of large (if underrepresented) countries from jamming
through decisions opposed by a persistently intense subset of (overrepresented but insufficiently numerous) small countries. Admittedly, that does
not leave a lot of decision space left—but no one said the making of an effective and democratic Euro-polity was going to be easy!

Obviously, it will be necessary to do a lot of detailed work on the specific weightings of votes within each *colegio* and on the probable lines of

cleavage that might form around specific issues and within specific committees. Only after the pertinent actors have done their simulations will it become apparent whether decision by concurrent majorities in three *colegii* might provide a common denominator that would not only assuage their worst fears but also permit them to move ahead on their common aspirations. So far, this is just a hunch, but I am convinced that this principle—along with those of pertinence and proportionality—might produce such a consensus. And if these changes in decision rules were implemented, along with at least some of the reform proposals for citizenship and representation, the outcome might not be "instant Euro-democracy," but it would provide a major impetus toward relegitimating the integration process by making it more accessible and accountable to the public.

AN EXCURSUS ON ENLARGEMENT AND ITS IMPACT
ON EXISTING AND PROSPECTIVE DECISION RULES

In this chapter, I have proposed a set of new principles concerning the distribution of votes and decision making in a more democratic European Union. One of the primary reasons that such changes may become necessary, however, has nothing to do with democratization as such. Rather, it relates to the imminent likelihood of enlargement, specifically the incorporation of a subset of countries in Eastern Europe and the Mediterranean. If one merely transposes the present arrangement for the EU of member states to future EUs with from seventeen to thirty-five members, the result would be a very substantial distortion of one of the EU's most important "foundational principles"—namely, its method for weighing the voting power of members according to their size of population. Under existing rules for qualified majority voting, it takes sixty-two of eighty-seven votes in the Council of Ministers—needless to say, voting as a single body—or 71 percent of the total to pass a measure and twenty-six votes of eighty-seven (30 percent) to veto one. This means that the five largest countries (Germany, France, the United Kingdom, Italy, and Spain) can veto decisions, but they cannot produce a qualified majority without help from either the five medium-size countries (Netherlands, Greece, Belgium, Hungary, and Sweden) or the five smallest countries (Austria, Denmark, Finland, Ireland, and Luxembourg).[20] Hence, the small and medium countries together cannot possibly form a qualified majority without the five largest ones, but they are able collectively to veto a decision. In other words, for the actual system to work effectively, cooperation is needed among all three size categories, and hence the results are likely to be consensual.[21]

However, extending this system to a total of, say, twenty-seven members would violate the existing size principle in two important ways. First, the ten prospective newcomers from Central and Eastern Europe countries (CEECs) would alone have a veto possibility, based on an aggregate population of 105 million, or just 22 percent of the EU's total population. Second, it would become possible to form a qualified majority only by adding the largest countries and the medium-size ones—not, as before, by adding the largest and either the medium or smallest ones. Any subsequent change in the direction of an absolute majority system would only further aggravate the problem by giving the medium and smallest countries, with only 26 percent of the population, a potential winning coalition over the seven largest countries with 74 percent of the EU's total population.

In contrast, a system that assigned votes in the Council of Ministers and seats in the European Parliament according to a uniform principle based in the square root of national populations has three advantages: (1) it would maintain the actual equilibrium and voting alternatives among the blocs of large, medium, and small countries and hence presumably benefit from existing criterion of legitimation; (2) it would provide a predictable ex ante "assignment" of voting weights and parliamentary seats for prospective members in all possible future compositions of the EU; and (3) it should defuse the fear among existing member states that a voting bloc could emerge from the new members from Central and Eastern Europe that might lead the EU into policy stalemate or a politics of subregional blackmail. I have called this arrangement *proportional proportionality*.

The second reform proposed here would go even further toward ensuring a consensual decision-making system and, nevertheless, allow the expanding EU to be make commitments binding on all against the resistance of individual states—even against the will of one of its largest members. An apposite device for doing this would involve dividing the votes in the Council of Ministers—putatively, the EU's upper chamber—into three *colegii* according to the relative size of member states. All "constitutional" decisions involving important substantive reforms, rule changes or the admission of new members would have to receive the support of all three *colegii*—instead of the present unanimity rule. Thus, no measure of major significance that was binding on all members could pass the council unless at least a *simple* majority of the *weighted* votes of small, medium, and large countries, voting separately according to proportional proportionality, approved it. For day-to-day matters, the present qualified majority or simple majority rules could be easily translated into the system of *colegii*, but in a less demanding fashion. Normal directives or EU laws would be approved if they obtained a simple-weighted majority in at least two of the *colegii*. In practice, this would mean that the (weighted) approval of *Colegio* I + *Colegio* II or *Colegio* I + *Colegio* III would suffice, whereas the opposition of any two *colegii* (including *Colegio* II + *Colegio* III) would amount to a veto. In the event of routine decisions currently governed by simple majority criteria, the same formula would apply, but only simple majorities would be required within each *colegio* and for the council as a whole. I have called this a system of *concurrent majorities*.

The Present System

As observed above, EU-15 works with a qualified majority voting procedure that requires sixty-two votes to be cast to reach a decision and twenty-six votes to veto a proposal. If one were to divide these fifteen member states—de facto and not (yet) de jure—into three *colegii* of five members each based on their relative size, we get the distribution illustrated in Table 4.1 (in absolute terms) and in Table 4.2 (in relative terms).[22] *Colegio* I of the five largest states has forty-eight votes, or 55

Table 4.1 The Present EU-15

		Pop.	Votes	Seats
I.	Germany	81.600.000	10	99
	United Kingdom	58.000.000	10	87
	France	58.000.000	10	87
	Italy	57.200.000	10	87
	Spain	39.600.000	8	64
II.	Netherlands	15.500.000	5	31
	Greece	10.500.000	5	25
	Belgium	10.100.000	5	25
	Portugal	9.800.000	5	25
	Sweden	8.800.000	4	22
III.	Austria	7.800.000	4	21
	Denmark	5.200.000	3	16
	Finland	5.100.000	3	16
	Ireland	3.600.000	3	15
	Luxembourg	400.000	2	6
	Total	371.200.000	87	626

percent; *Colegio* II of the middle-size states has twenty-four votes, or 28 percent; and *Colegio* III of the five smallest has fifteen votes, or 17 percent of the total eighty-seven votes that can be cast. Any decision that receives a qualified majority in a *colegio* automatically receives all of the weighted votes of that *colegio*. Under such an arrangement, with the qualified majority established at sixty-two votes (71 percent), a positive decision can be reached either by adding the votes of *Colegii* I + II or *Colegii* I + III, but not by adding *Colegii* II + III. However, any two *colegii* can, if they vote in the same direction, veto a decision.

It is my assumption that the existing system is not merely an accidental product but reflects an underlying principle that serves to legitimate decision making among national states of very considerable diversity in their respective populations, geographical area and market power. This basic (if unstated) "size principle" should be conserved in the future as the EU incorporates new members.

Table 4.2 Present Relative Weights

	Pop.	Votes	Seats
Colegio I	294.400.000 (79%)	48 (55%)	424 (68%)
Colegio II	54.700.000 (15%)	24 (28%)	128 (20%)
Colegio III	22.100.000 (6%)	15 (17%)	74 (12%)

The enlargement from EU-12 to EU-15 already produced several important crises. Great Britain bitterly resented any decrease in its potential veto power and envisaged a dangerous future in which "spendthrift" southerners could outvote "abstemious" northerners. Inversely, the Spanish government wanted to prevent the disappearance of the potential "Mediterranean veto," according to which Spain (eight votes), plus France or Italy (ten votes each), plus Portugal or Greece (five votes each), could reach the twenty-three votes necessary to veto any council decision.[23] The so-called Ionannina compromise reflected the necessity to assure some countries that the decrease in their relative voting strength weight due to an eventual increase in membership would be taken into account, even if informally. In this particular compromise, it was decided that whenever any group of states representing twenty-three to twenty-five votes would oppose a decision to be taken by qualified majority, their negative opinion would be taken into account, even if these countries lacked the capacity (or will) to cast a formal veto, and the council would try to find a satisfactory solution which could receive at least sixty-five votes (instead of the sixty-two necessary).[24]

Whether this particular solution will endure, the pattern of conflict behind it illustrates very well the problems that are bound to emerge with greater intensity in the future. Enlargement to the east (and, to a lesser extent, to the south with Malta and Cyprus) has to involve states with two characteristics that are most adverse to the present EU voting system: (1) either they are small in population and hence would have the net effect of increasing the already very considerable overrepresentation of small countries, or (2) they come from a geographically and culturally compact part of Europe and hence threaten to contribute further to the already considerable fear of regional bloc formation.[25] The emergence of northern, eastern, and southern or Mediterranean bloc voting could well unleash a broader uncertainty about where the "center of gravity" or "core area" of Europe really was—and disrupt the current (implicit) consensus on Franco-German duopoly. The present system has, so far, proven to be tolerable, despite its gross disproportionality at the superior and inferior extremes of country size (see Table 4.2: at present, 79 percent of the population has 55 percent of the votes), but it could be disrupted if overshadowed or displaced by regional solidarities.

The Search for Alternatives

Actors seem aware of the potential serious destabilizing effect of maintaining and extending the present system to future configurations of the EU. It was one of the major preoccupations of decision makers within the so-called reflection group that prepared the Intergovernmental Conference

(IGC) on political reform. However, progress in this matter was nonexistent—because of the reluctance of member states to consider any alteration of their relative power under a new voting and decision-making system. A variety of formulae was proposed without success, mainly because they have not been able to offer a system that is both effective and legitimate.

An examination of several alternative systems, all derived from public choice theory, has recently been carried out by Torsten Peters.[26] The first one (the Shapley-Shubik Index) considers which country would be pivotal to the determination of winning coalitions, according to a given order of voting. The second (based on the Banzhaf Index) examines potential coalitions, instead of permutations, and attempts to find which countries can turn winning coalitions into losing coalitions by changing the direction of their vote. According to that system, larger countries can be pivotal more often than smaller ones. Finally, the third uses Holler's Index in an effort to correct what its author considers an overestimation of larger country capabilities inherent in the preceding two indexes and proposes a solution which results in a more equal distribution of weighted votes.

Peters then confronts the three indices with four different voting reform scenarios, while holding constant the number of states at fifteen. The results show clearly that any reform that reduces the number of votes necessary for a majority to be formed will only marginally reduce the power of small states. Furthermore, if the requisite majority were reduced to a simple majority and, simultaneously, the number of countries required to form a majority is also decreased (to nine or eight), the power of small states would even increase compared to the actual system.

In other words, the commonsense solution to future enlargement (i.e., to reduce the number of votes and countries necessary to form winning majorities) would have precisely the opposite effect, if—as will definitely be the case—new members are predominantly small in size. In an EU with twenty-seven members, decisions by simple majority would definitely be easier than by qualified majority, but they could be taken by member states representing only 26 percent of the EU's then total population (i.e., by 122,200,000 against 355,600,000 inhabitants). If, in reaction to this prospect, the twenty-seven future members decide to maintain the present qualified majority system, the picture is not much more promising, since the Eastern European latecomers (Bulgaria, the Czech Republic, Estonia, Hungary, Latvia, Lithuania, Poland, Romania, Slovakia, Slovenia), with 41 votes of 132 and a population of 22 percent, would have a potential clear veto on all new measures.[27]

A System with Concurrent Majorities and Proportional Proportionality

The combination of a decision-making arrangement based on three *colegii* and the weighting of votes according to the square root of popula-

Table 4.3 EU-27 with Present System

	Countries	Votes
I.	Germany, U.K., France and Italy	10
	Spain and Poland	8
	Romania	6
II.	Netherlands, Greece, Czech Republic, Belgium, Hungary and Portugal	5
	Sweden, Bulgaria and Austria	4
III.	Slovakia, Denmark, Finland, Lithuania, Ireland and Latvia	3
	Slovenia, Estonia, Cyprus, Luxembourg and Malta	2

tion appears (to me) to be an optimal solution that would keep the EU system working according to its present principles and allow it to adjust to any future configuration.[28] Let us see why.

Let us begin with the premise that any reform should respect *grosso modo* the actual system of relative weights among the larger, medium, and smaller countries. We are looking for a device whereby the largest countries would still need the support of *either* the small or the medium-size countries to obtain a binding majority. This is a system that guarantees the right to preeminence of the large countries while preventing them from "tyrannizing" the others. Also, since their concurrence is necessary, it makes it worthwhile for medium and small states to remain within the EU—rather than to "free ride" on its periphery. But the peculiarity of the system is that it also gives a fair (i.e., a proportionately proportionate) share of voting power to the medium and small states. Together, they cannot impose their will on the large countries, but together they can veto any proposal.

The obvious solution is to find a device or devices that could permanently ensure the reproduction of such decision-making principles, no matter how many members the EU decides to admit in the future. An examination of the effect of weighing states' voting power according to the square root of their populations demonstrates the viability of such a system in a Europe of seventeen members, if and when the two small states of Malta and Cyprus are admitted; a Europe of twenty-one, by adding the Visegrad Four; and a Europe of twenty-seven that would include the ten Eastern European and Baltic states, but not the CIS, the Ukraine, Croatia, Serbia-Montenegro, Macedonia, Albania, or Moldova. It even works with a mega-Europe of thirty-five countries and 572 million inhabitants!

This can be accomplished by combining a qualified majoritarian system at the EU level with a qualified majority-bloc voting system at the level of the *colegii*. The qualified majority rule would still hold globally because it would continue to be necessary for any directive to obtain 71 percent of the weighted votes for a proposal to become binding. Larger countries would still have to ally with either medium or small countries to obtain that 71 percent. Also in common with the present system, the medium and smaller countries could veto a proposal agreed to by the larger countries, if they voted together.

The basic difference is that voting in the council would also take place *within* each of the three *colegii* under a modified first-past-the-post system. Any coalition of countries whose weighted votes approved a directive/law within a *colegio* would carry all the votes of that *colegio* to the next stage.[29] As we shall see later in greater detail, this produces two net advantages. First, it would break up the possibility of forming dominant or veto blocs based on geographic or cultural regions, since the northerners, southerners, and easterners would be distributed among the three *colegii* according to their relative size. By itself, this should suppress the fears derived from the typical instability of triadic systems that the prospect of three regional groups would surely unleash. Second, within each *colegio*, the range of possible coalitions should be much more varied, permitting countries to align according to their particular preferences with regard to the policy issue at stake, rather than according to relatively fixed strategic calculations of relative power and status. For example, in EU-27, *Colegio* I would have seven countries (see Table 4.3). Germany plus the U.K, France, and Italy would have an enabling majority, but Spain, Poland, and Romania could also be in the winning coalition if they could convince any two of the four above to join them. In *Colegio* II with nine middle-size countries, any five countries could form the necessary majority, since they are so close to each other according to the size principle. Finally, in *Colegio* III with its eleven small members, the possible winning coalitions would range from any four of the largest to the five smallest plus at least two of the larger ones. The combinations are thus quite diverse—one is tempted to say *pluralistic*—but relations among the *colegii* should ensure a strong bias toward consensual solutions rather than the winner-take-all mentality of simple or even qualified majority systems in a single representative body.

To become a law or directive of the EU, a proposal would have to obtain a concurrent majority (CM) of 71 percent of the council votes as a whole *and* a simple majority in at least two of the *colegii*. For matters of constitutional importance, the criteria could be strengthened to include the requirement that a simple majority of the weighted votes in all three *colegii* would be necessary.

The entire system rests on proportional proportionality (PP) derived from the square root of each country's population. I am assuming that this universalistic standard, while it deviates from the usual "one person, one vote" criteria applied in virtually all liberal democracies, would prove acceptable to the EU as a whole. In effect, what PP would ensure is that representation would be equal for similar *proportions* of the citizenry of different size political units. For example, 10 percent of the population of Luxembourg (40,000 persons) would have approximately the same voting weight/number of seats as 10 percent of the population of Germany (816,000 persons). Not only can this criterion be defended normatively—provided all agree that both Luxembourg and Germany deserve to persist in their present territorial/demographic configuration—but it is a more objective and easy-to-measure basis for differentiation than level of development, geographic location, religious conviction, or any other cultural trait. Europeans have long lived in national societies of different size, and this is predictably associated with varying intensities of feeling with regard to such things as language use, cultural preferences, institutional peculiarities, and so forth. If the larger countries refuse to recognize this proportionately fair criterion for over- and underrepresentation and insist on strictly numerical equality, any peaceful and voluntary effort to democratize the Euro-polity is bound to fail.

If the proposed PP system where applied to the present EU-15 and the number of votes in the Council of Ministers remained unchanged at eighty-seven, the previous system maintains its basic features—which is precisely the goal we have been seeking. Germany's votes would be increased to twelve (from ten) and Greece, Belgium, Portugal, and Luxembourg would lose a single vote (see Table 4.4).[30] A quick look at Table 4.5 shows how little variation in votes the new system would produce.[31] Thanks to the *colegii* arrangement, it would still be necessary for one of the two smaller units to enter into a coalition with *Colegio* I for any measure to pass. Moreover, as we have discussed earlier, coalitions within each *colegio* should be very fluid over time and across issues, given that any three of their five members can form a simple majority and obtain all the votes of that *colegio*.[32] Now, let us see how the system would work when faced with three possible future scenarios.

The Proposed System Applied to Future EU Enlargements

EU-17

Let us first speculate with what would happen should Malta and Cyprus enter the EU-15 as planned (see Table 4.6). Under the present system, both countries, one with four hundred thousand and the other with seven hundred thousand inhabitants, would be entitled to two votes in the coun-

Table 4.4 EU-15 with PP and CM

		New Votes	Old Votes	New Seats	Old Seats
I.	Germany	12	10	88	99
	United Kingdom	10	10	74	87
	France	10	10	74	87
	Italy	10	10	73	87
	Spain	8	8	61	64
II.	Netherlands	5	5	38	31
	Greece	4	5	31	25
	Belgium	4	5	31	25
	Portugal	4	5	30	25
	Sweden	4	4	29	22
III.	Austria	4	4	27	21
	Denmark	3	3	22	16
	Finland	3	3	22	16
	Ireland	3	3	18	15
	Luxembourg	1	2	6	6
	Total	85	87	624	626

cil. This would quite substantially alter the voting strength of the small member states since, by adding only slightly more than one million inhabitants to the EU (0.3 percent), it would increase their collective votes by 27 percent (i.e., from fifteen to nineteen). Faced with that prospect, the fifteen could opt to do nothing. The subset of large countries could still not be overridden by a potential coalition of medium and smaller countries, and they would still need the votes of one or the other "size blocs." Needless to say, the (implicit) southern or Mediterranean veto would be strengthened to the delight of Spain and Italy and the dismay of Britain and the Scandinavians.

If PP were applied to EU-17, winning majorities could be formed without including as many of the larger countries. The twelve medium- and small-size members would have 42 percent—if they voted together—and the five large ones would have the remaining 58 percent votes in the coun-

Table 4.5 EU-15 Present and Proposed Votes and Seats by Colegii

	New Votes	Old Votes	New Seats	Old Seats
Colegio I	50 (59%)	48 (55%)	370 (59%)	424 (68%)
Colegio II	21 (25%)	24 (28%)	159 (26%)	128 (20%)
Colegio III	14 (16%)	15 (17%)	95 (15%)	74 (12%)

Chapter 4

Table 4.6 EU-17 with PP and CM

		Population	Votes	Seats
I.	Germany	81.600.000	14	96
	United Kingdom	58.000.000	12	81
	France	58.000.000	12	81
	Italy	57.200.000	11	80
	Spain	39.600.000	10	67
II.	Netherlands	15.500.000	6	42
	Greece	10.500.000	5	34
	Belgium	10.100.000	5	34
	Portugal	9.800.000	5	33
	Sweden	8.800.000	5	32
	Austria	7.800.000	4	30
III.	Denmark	5.200.000	3	24
	Finland	5.100.000	3	24
	Ireland	3.600.000	3	20
	Cyprus	700.000	1	9
	Luxembourg	400.000	1	7
	Malta	400.000	1	7
	Total	372.300.000	101	701

cil.[33] Of course, according to the rules of the Council of Ministers, it would still be highly unlikely that its members would pass anything that could negatively affect the group as a whole, and, on constitutional issues, this group would still have a veto. The strongest argument in favor of introducing the reform already for EU-17 is that it would serve to familiarize members with their new voting weights and allow them to begin experimenting with the formation of coalitions within each of the *colegii*. Moreover, this would set a precedent under relatively easy conditions for negotiation since the immediate impact would be so negligible. A very important and contentious issue that is bound to plague much more complex enlargements in the future would have been resolved in a way that is universal, predictable and defensible in terms of democratic theory. Each potential member state would know before it entered into negotiations what its weighted vote would be and where it would fit within the decision-making procedures as a whole. The "shadow of the future" will have been clarified considerably, if not dissipated altogether—and the conflicts surrounding eventual inclusion and exclusion should (hopefully) turn to other, more substantive matters.

If the EU were to adopt PP and CM, it would also be desirable to further simplify its rules. For example, the member states would be well advised to set the number of weighted votes in the Council of Ministers at a fixed sum—say, one hundred—and make it even easier for everyone to calculate the possible impact of any enlargement.[34] This way, all eventual changes in membership would result in a (predictable) redistribution of weighted votes among the preexisting members, as well as the assignment of new "quotas" to those just entering. Under the *colegii* system, countries would be assigned to one of the three subgroups according to the size of their respective populations.[35] If it was felt to be desirable to keep the *colegii* more or less equal in terms of the number of members, specific countries could even be promoted from medium to large or small to medium status, although in so elevating themselves they would lose some of their proportional clout. Perhaps, one could allow them the choice of remaining a relatively large fish in a small pond or becoming a small fish in a larger pond! In any case, all of the fish—no matter how small—would get at least one vote.[36]

For EU-17, the results of PP and CM would be as follows, according to Table 4.6: (1) The "big guys" in *Colegio* I would have 58 percent of the votes, and any three among them could win or veto a decision; (2) in *Colegio* II, with 29 percent of the total votes, the potential winning or vetoing coalitions seem indeterminant: Austria plus any three of the others or the Netherlands allied with any two among Greece, Belgium, Portugal or Ireland; (3) *Colegio* III would only have 12 percent of council votes and a considerable variety of potential combinations: the smallest three plus any two among Denmark, Finland, or Ireland could veto, as could either of these three "big small countries" by joining the three smallest ones (Cyprus, Luxembourg or Malta). The overall principle is protected, however. It would still take a majority in *Colegio* I plus either *Colegio* II or III to win, and the combination of *Colegio* II and III can still veto.

EU-21

Now, the institutions of the EU are being put to a stiffer test, that of incorporating the three of the so-called Visegrad Four: the Czech Republic, Hungary, Poland, plus Slovenia (see Table 4.7).[37]

The basic rule of qualified majority would still hold, since *Colegio* I (with Poland as its sixth Great European Power) would have 54 percent of the total votes, *Colegio* II (now joined by the Czech Republic and Hungary) would have 29 percent, and *Colegio* III (with incoming Slovenia and descending Austria) 17 percent. Thus, the small and medium countries could veto but not decide, whereas the largest countries would still need one of the two small *colegii* to reach the necessary majority. Also, coalitions within each *colegio* would be potentially quite varied—at least without reference to any specific substantive issue.[38] In *Colegio* I, the potential threat of a majority bloc composed exclusively of Mediterranean

Table 4.7 EU-21 with PP and CM

		Population	Votes	Seats
I.	Germany	81.600.000	11	78
	United Kingdom	58.800.000	10	66
	France	57.800.000	9	66
	Italy	57.200.000	9	65
	Spain	39.600.000	8	54
	Poland	38.400.000	8	54
II.	Netherlands	15.500.000	5	34
	Greece	10.500.000	4	28
	Czech Republic	10.300.000	4	28
	Belgium	10.100.000	4	28
	Hungary	10.100.000	4	28
	Portugal	9.800.000	4	27
	Sweden	8.800.000	4	26
III.	Austria	7.800.000	3	24
	Denmark	5.200.000	3	20
	Finland	5.100.000	3	20
	Ireland	3.600.000	2	16
	Slovenia	1.900.000	1	10
	Cyprus	700.000	1	6
	Luxembourg	400.000	1	5
	Malta	400.000	1	5
	Total	433.600.000	99	698

countries (France + Italy + Spain) is dissipated. Either the smallest four or the biggest three among the Great Powers can form a winning coalition. In *Colegio* II, the picture has become even more varied: of seven countries, any four could produce a majority and the only stable alliance one might imagine would involve its four older members (Greece, Netherlands, Portugal, and Belgium). This is not very likely given their behavior in the EU to date. In *Colegio* III, the biggest four countries could dominate, but so also could the smallest three if they could convince any three of the five remaining ones. Thus, the system of relative weights within *colegii* plus the first-past-the post bloc voting provision assigned to each *colegio* should guarantee respect for one of the foundations of the present EU system, despite a major change in the number of players. There are still the internal checks and balances between different countries grouped by size, but no greater a propensity for stalemate or blackmail by hardcore recalcitrants.

EU-27

Now let us see what happens to the properties of the EU system when PP and CM are applied to what many regard as its most likely final configuration—at some indefinite moment in the twenty-first century (see Table 4.8). Besides the Visegrad Four (now with Slovakia), two Southeastern European countries (Bulgaria and Romania) and the three Baltic states have all signed association agreements with the EU. No doubt, their inferior economic conditions (not to mention the problematic consolidation of democracy in several of these countries) might defer their entry for some time; nevertheless, the EU's formal stance is that they will all become members.

Table 4.8 EU-27 with PP and CM

		Population	Votes	Seats
I.	Germany	81.600.000	10	67
	United Kingdom	58.000.000	8	56
	France	58.000.000	8	56
	Italy	57.200.000	8	56
	Spain	39.600.000	7	47
	Poland	38.400.000	7	46
	Romania	22.800.000	5	35
II.	Netherlands	15.500.000	4	29
	Greece	10.500.000	3	24
	Czech Republic	10.300.000	3	24
	Belgium	10.100.000	3	23
	Hungary	10.100.000	3	23
	Portugal	9.800.000	3	23
	Sweden	8.800.000	3	22
	Bulgaria	8.800.000	3	22
	Austria	7.800.000	3	21
III.	**Slovakia**	5.400.000	2	17
	Denmark	5.200.000	2	17
	Finland	5.100.000	2	17
	Lithuania	3.700.000	2	14
	Ireland	3.600.000	2	14
	Latvia	2.600.000	2	12
	Slovenia	1.900.000	1	10
	Estonia	1.500.000	1	9
	Cyprus	700.000	1	6
	Luxembourg	400.000	1	5
	Malta	400.000	1	5
	Total	477.800.000	98	700

And this is where and when the decision-making problems will surely become especially acute, unless the existing rules are changed. If not, as we have discussed above, the new "Eastern bloc" of ten countries (of twenty-seven) would be so overrepresented that collectively they could veto all initiatives within the council (while only having 22 percent of the EU-27's total population). This is presumably the menacing shadow of the future that all existing members have an interest in avoiding.

And the proposed combination of PP and CM would do just that—without resorting to any explicitly discriminatory treatment. Especially if it could be implemented early enough, its effects should be perceived as generic and fair. It would tend to impede the formation of any geographically or culturally based subregional veto, just as it would continue to encourage the larger countries to take into account the preferences of their medium and small partners.

In EU-27 with PP and CM, *Colegio* I joined by Romania would have a weight of 54 percent; *Colegio* II, now with Bulgaria in its ranks, would have 29 percent; and *Colegio* III with four new members (the Baltic Republics + Slovakia) would have 17 percent. With the qualified majority remaining at 71 percent and the prospective veto at 30 percent, all of the checks and balances discussed earlier would continue to function. Within each *colegio*, a considerable variety of winning and vetoing combinations have become possible; moreover, they do not cluster by either level of development or geocultural region. In *Colegio* I, a coalition of Germany plus the next three "biggies" or one formed by the smallest three plus any two of the four largest countries would be able to pass directives and win all of its fifty-three votes. In *Colegio* II, any five of the nine countries composing it could produce a simple majority and obtain its fifteen votes. In *Colegio* III, the necessary majority would be nine of seventeen votes. Its five eastern and Baltic members would have to attract either Denmark, Finland, Ireland, Cyprus, Luxembourg,or Malta to their ranks in order to produce a majority—and even then they would still have to join with a majority in either *Colegio* I or *Colegio* II to enact their preferred measures. Most likely, the pattern of voting in *Colegio* III with its more numerous (and one must add very heterogenous in terms of level of development) membership should be quite varied with possible majorities coming from any four of its two-vote members plus one of its five one-vote governments, while all of the five smallest countries in that *colegio* would need at least two of the larger ones to reach an effective majority.

EU-35

We are now pushing the envelope of possible "Europes." And no one questions that the issue of such a mega-enlargement lies far in the future. EU-35 would include all countries that, for one reason or another and with one degree of seriousness or another, have expressed or might express in the future a desire to enter the European Union. These prospective members include Turkey, the Federal Republic of Yugoslavia (Serbia and Montenegro), Switzerland, Croatia, Norway, Macedonia, Albania, and Iceland (see Table 4.9).[39]

Table 4.9 EU-35 with PP and CM

		Population	Votes	Seats
I.	Germany	81.600.000	8	54
	Turkey	61.900.000	7	47
	United Kingdom	58.000.000	7	46
	France	58.000.000	7	46
	Italy	57.200.000	6	45
	Spain	39.600.000	5	38
	Poland	38.400.000	5	37
	Romania	22.800.000	4	29
II.	Netherlands	15.500.000	3	24
	Yugoslavia	10.800.000	3	20
	Greece	10.500.000	3	19
	Czech Republic	10.300.000	3	19
	Belgium	10.100.000	3	19
	Hungary	10.100.000	3	19
	Portugal	9.800.000	3	19
	Bulgaria	8.800.000	3	18
	Sweden	8.800.000	3	18
III.	Austria	7.800.000	2	17
	Switzerland	7.200.000	2	16
	Slovakia	5.400.000	2	14
	Denmark	5.200.000	2	14
	Finland	5.100.000	2	14
	Croatia	4.500.000	2	13
	Norway	4.300.000	2	12
	Lithuania	3.700.000	2	12
	Ireland	3.600.000	2	11
	Albania	3.400.000	2	11
	Latvia	2.600.000	1	10
	Macedonia	2.200.000	1	9
	Slovenia	1.900.000	1	8
	Estonia	1.500.000	1	7
	Cyprus	700.000	1	5
	Luxembourg	400.000	1	4
	Malta	400.000	1	4
	Iceland	300.000	1	3
	Total	572.400.000	104	701

Table 4.9 shows that the application of PP and CM to a putative Europolity of this enormous scale (572 million inhabitants according to present figures!) would not produce radically different potential political outcomes, even if one could question whether any mechanism of democratic representation and accountability could function effectively for such a demographically numerous and culturally varied population. To demonstrate that EU-35 is possible is not the same thing as arguing that it would be desirable.

The increase in number of countries belonging to *Colegio* III by five does not alter substantially the situation with respect to EU-27 as described earlier. *Colegio* I would get just one new member (Turkey) but only diminish its proportion of the total council votes from 54 percent to 47 percent. Again, it would only be able to reach a qualified majority with the help of winning majorities among the medium or small states in either *Colegio* II or *Colegio* III. The former would have 26 percent of the votes (as opposed to 28 percent in EU-27) with 17 percent of the expanded European population. The latter would now have a total of 28 of the 104 votes in the council, up from 17 of 98 in the EU's previous configuration. Moreover, its 27 percent would correspond to sixty million Europeans, while *Colegio* II with almost ninety-five million would have one less vote. Despite this anomaly, by making voting concurrent among the three *colegii*, its effect is nullified. As before, the PP and CM system works to prevent the larger states from being placed in a minority and to ensure that the medium and smaller states will not be marginalized or ignored. Those eight Great European Powers with 73 percent of the total population would have to be content with 47 percent of the voting power, while the rest of weighted votes would be almost equally distributed between the nine medium and the eighteen small states.

*   *   *

I am convinced that the combination of proportional proportionality and concurrent majority offers the best solution for allocating weighted votes and for making binding decisions in the Council of Ministers of a continuously enlarging European Union. Its basic principles are consistent with those already in use and defensible in terms of democratic theory; its calculations are simple, predictable, and open-ended; its procedures should promote flexibility and consensual decision making; its results are likely to be sufficiently fair and other regarding to encourage those who are outside the EU to join it and those who are inside the EU to remain within it.

A SHORT EXCURSUS ON THE EUROPEAN PARLIAMENT

The critical (and democratically concerned) reader will surely have noticed that I have given scant attention to the European Parliament (EP) in this discussion of possible reforms in the rules of decision making and voting. The observant reader, however, will have noticed that in each of the tables in chapter 4 I have displayed the effect of applying proportional proportionality to the distribution of seats in that body. In these tables, he or she can readily see how various future enlargements of the EU might be translated into changes in the distribution of seats for Members of the European Parliament (MEPs), if the method of weighing according to the square root of the country's total population were applied and if the eventual reformers were sensible enough to limit the total size of the EP to seven hundred MEPs. I see no reason that, if the principle of proportionate proportionality is acceptable for distributing votes in the Council of Ministers, it should not be used for the same purpose in the parliament. A quick perusal of the results it produces from EU-15 all the way to EU-35 would show that—as intended—it overrepresents the smallest countries, but it does not radically alter the present system. Perhaps its major difficulty would have to be faced initially since such "biggies" as Germany (eighty-eight from ninety-nine), the United Kingdom (seventy-four from eighty-seven), France (seventy-four from eighty-seven) and Italy (seventy-three from eighty-seven) would have to face a considerable reduction in their number of seats. It should be noted, however, that these large delegations could still be expected to wield a considerable amount of informal influence via party channels and that, in any case, the EP is not designed to represent "national" populations as such but individual citizens.

What would not be appropriate would be to transfer the system of concurrent majorities to the European Parliament. The main purpose of the EP is to insert within the political process of the EU a different (i.e., "partisan") mode of representation, one that can potentially moderate and counteract the effects of representation according to national states. In the EP, it is the individual citizen that is being (indirectly) brought into the process through the internal divisions of each country's party system and (eventually) through the formation of partisan alliances along transnational lines of cleavage and solidarity. Representatives in the EP are not expected to vote along national lines, and it would make no sense to force them to do so through the concurrent majority system.

I can only think of two instances in which its division into three *colegii* might make some sense: (1) if the EP were granted the power to force the resignation of individual commissioners and if these commissioners were nominated according to the *colegii* system, then it would seem proper that only the MEPs from the countries in the *colegio* that initially proposed the candidate should have a definitive voice in determining whether that commissioner should remain in his or her position; (2) if it were felt that, for very significant decisions such as major rules changes or the admission of new members, the existing "collegial" guarantees embedded in the Council of Ministers were insufficient to ensure legitimacy before mass publics, then it might be advisable to require that these decisions be approved by a concurrent majority of MEPs grouped by country size in the three *colegii*, although to me this seems superfluous.

Otherwise, the procedures of the European Parliament should be as close as possible to those of a "normal" (i.e., national) parliament with its self-elected leadership, its party caucuses, its standing committees, its majoritarian decision making, and so forth. Admittedly, this will demand some major reforms in the future, especially with regard to the nature and uniformity of its electoral system, but to discuss them here would take us far beyond the intent of this short excursus.

NOTES

1. Not the least of these ambiguities is whether the so-called Luxembourg Compromise of 1965–96 is still in effect. If so, it would permit any member country to veto unilaterally any decision that it felt harmed its "vital national interests." It was last used overtly in 1985 when Germany applied it (with French support) to retain high price supports for its grain producers. The French government's last-minute blackmail during the GATT negotiations of 1993–94 may have been another case in point. Keith Middlemas, *Orchestrating Europe* (London: Fontana, 1995), 291.

2. Perhaps more relevant is the fact that since further enlargement involves smaller countries (except for Poland) and since these countries are likely to be overrepresented in EU institutions, the relative weight of the larger countries (Germany, France, Italy, Great Britain, and Spain) would inexorably diminish. This "shadow of the future" should incline them to be interested in a change in the rules, even one that could offer substantial concessions to their smaller brethren.

3. The most obvious case is the Committee of Permanent Representatives (COREPER), which prepares all the documents for the Council of Ministers. Its decision rules do not seem to have been formalized, and, in any case, its deliberations are secret. Lionel Barber, the *Financial Times* correspondent in Brussels, has estimated that 90 percent of the decisions with regard to EU directives are taken in this forum. "The Men Who Run Europe," *Financial Times,* March 11–12, 1995, p. 1.

4. This number is according to the calculations of the commission in its *Report on the Operation of the Treaty of European Union,* SEC(95), 731 (May 10, 1995), 23. One of the few accomplishments of the Treaty of Amsterdam (1997) was to simplify these procedures somewhat.

5. It should be noted, however, that in the case of initiatives coming from the council and the parliament, the commission is not formally obligated to respond with a concrete proposal.

6. This typology first appeared in Philippe C. Schmitter and Terry Karl, "The Types of Democracy Emerging in Southern and Eastern Europe and South and Central America," in *Bound to Change: Consolidating Democracy in Central Europe,* ed. Peter Volten (New York: Institute for East-West Security Studies, 1992), 42–68.

7. *Democracies: Patterns of Majoritarian and Consensus Government* (New Haven, Conn.: Yale University Press, 1984).

8. According to a recent report of the commission, there are no fewer than fifty-five matters for which unanimity is still required! European Commission, *Report on the Operation of the Treaty on European Union,* SEC(95) 731 (May 10, 1995).

9. In addition to the articles cited in chapter 3, n. 12, by Schmitter and Streeck and Traxler and Schmitter, see the general survey by J. Greenwood and K. Ronit, "Interest Groups in the European Community: Newly Emerging Dynamics and Forms," *Western European Politics* 17, no. 1 (January 1994): 31–52.

10. For a similar proposal (but put to a somewhat different purpose), see Justus Lipsius, "The 1996 IGC," *European Law Review* 20, no. 3 (1995): 235–67.

Also see Gerda Falkner and Michael Nentwich, *European Union: Democratic Perspectives after 1996* (Vienna: Service Fachverlang, 1995), 87.

Note that it should be possible to assign membership to *colegii* in a flexible fashion so that they would tend to divide the entire membership into more or less equal thirds. Countries approaching the upper or lower limit in terms of the size of their citizenry could be moved up or down as the case may be in order that one *colegio* would not become too large and thereby dilute the significance of any one member's vote.

11. It has been estimated that if the present proportions were to prevail and the EU were to expand to twenty-eight members, the EP would have to have almost nine hundred members. Justus Lipsius, "The 1996 IGC," *European Law Journal* 3 (1995): 37.

12. Together with José Torreblanca, I have written an excursus at the end of this chapter that demonstrates the relative effect of different prospective EUs—of fifteen, seventeen, twenty-one, and thirty-five—on the distribution of weighted votes in the council and the number of seats in the EP.

13. It seems highly likely that the unanimity rule would never be completely abolished within the Euro-polity. It will probably persist for future changes in major constitutional rules and may even be left in the present limbo with regard to any issue that threatens "the vital national interests of a member state"—although fellow members may increasingly insist on some role in defining the bona fides of such an assertion. Invoking it to protect one's cereal producers or moviemakers from "unfair" foreign competition may no longer be tolerated.

14. This concept of "concurrent majority" originated with the ideas of American political theorist-cum-politician, John C. Calhoun, where it was put to the unfortunate precedent of defending the minority slave-holding states of the South of the United States against the rising majoritarian tide of the northern, non-slave-holding, states. See Calhoun's *A Disquisition on Government* (New York: Peter Smith, 1943), originally published in 1853. The discussion of concurrent majority can be found on pp. 28*ff*.

15. If this seems complicated, it should be noted that there is no reason that the three *colegii* would ever have to meet separately, much less have any staff or institutional framework of their own. The council would meet, deliberate, and vote as a whole, except that the tallies would be compiled separately.

16. This would also do away with the two "specters" that have been haunting the Euro-polity, namely, that with enlargement (1) it will become technically possible for a minority of the European citizenry to override a majority, and (2) depending on their numbers, it will become technically possible for the new eastern members to block any legislation. By dividing the Euro-polity into three *colegii* according to size, it would no longer be feasible to override the preferences of the largest countries (provided a majority of them agreed), and the votes of the prospective eastern members would be distributed according to relative size, presumably with Poland being placed in the large category, the Baltic Republics, Cyprus, Malta, Slovakia, and Slovenia going to the smallest, with the remainder—Hungary, the Czech Republic, Romania, Bulgaria, and, perhaps, Croatia—going into the middle one.

17. This point presumes something that I will not develop in greater detail—namely, the EP simplifies its decision-making procedures, and that "codecision" in which it and the council have coequal powers and must cooperate at all stages of the legislative procedure will become the norm in the future, with the "assent" procedure largely confined to admission of new members and approval of nominees for major administrative and judicial offices.

18. Note that this argument presumes that presidentialism, especially in the form of popular election of the president of the commission, would be utterly inappropriate for the emerging Euro-polity. Whether it might be desirable to have a more or less symbolic head of polity as is usual in strong parliamentary or monarchic regimes is a different matter.

19. *Democracy and Its Critics* (New Haven, Conn.: Yale University Press, 1989), 52 et seq.

20. The Treaty (Article 148) establishes the qualified majority at sixty-two votes whenever a commission proposal is involved and sixty-two votes representing at least ten member states in the rest of the cases. The clear intention is to avoid "government by size"—that is, that the largest eight member states acting together would be able to make rules binding all fifteen.

21. It should be noted that this "hidden" rule operates whether or not the actual voting patterns vary according to the size of country. They are, so to speak, embedded in the context of voting in the EU's Council of Ministers and presumed to affect the behavior of member states by anticipation and habit; that is, they "structure" actor preferences in advance. In any case, since council voting is "opaque," there is no systematic and reliable way of verifying present behavior and hence of predicting how the change of rules I propose will affect future behavior—which is not to say that those who have been directly involved will not be able to estimate their effect.

For a comprehensive assessment of how the council operates, see Fiona Hayes-Renshaw and Helen Wallace, "Executive Power in the European Union: The Functions and Limits of the Council of Ministers," *Journal of European Public Policy* 2, no. 4 (December 1995): 559–82. They estimate that contentious issues actually leading to formal voting by ministers—whether by unanimity or qualified majority—only amount to 10 to 15 percent of the total. The rest is settled consensually by senior officials at one level or another (p. 562). They also conclude that they could find "no systematic cleavage between smaller and larger members" (p. 577), which does not, I believe, argue against the utility of the *colegii* system I propose. My purpose is to preclude and pre-empt conflict among different-sized countries, not to mirror or institutionalize this line of cleavage.

For the conclusion that all previous enlargements have enhanced the relative voting power of smaller EU members, see Madeleine O. Hosli, "Admission of European Free Trade Association States to the European Community: Effects on Voting Power in the European Community Council of Ministers," *International Organization* 47, no. 4 (Autumn 1993): 631.

22. Population figures for all the tables have been extracted from 1996 *Keesing's World Record of Events*, which uses United Nations data.

23. Prior to the Nordic enlargement, qualified majority stood at fifty-four votes and veto at twenty-three, with a total number of votes of seventy-six. Spain argued that Norway, Finland, Sweden, and Denmark, with only twenty-three million inhabitants, would have thirteen votes at the council, whereas Spain would count on only eight votes having a population of thirty-nine million. With the support of the United Kingdom, it fought unsuccessfully for new veto rights to be awarded according to population criteria—more specifically, whenever coalitions of two big and one small country representing a hundred million inhabitants opposed a particular decision. Not coincidentally, Spain plus France or Italy plus Greece or Portugal made up that figure (see *El País,* March 2, 1994, p. 4).

24. Council decision of March 19, 1994, amended on January 1, 1995. See *Official Journal of the European Communities*, No. C 105 of April 13, 1994 and No. C 1 of January 1, 1995.

25. As observed in n. 21, the issue is not whether the eastern (or, for that matter, the Mediterranean or the northern) countries really form a voting bloc but whether they might be anticipated to do so on specific issues or at some specific moment in the future. Moreover, the present system offers some perverse incentives. For example, the former Czechoslovak Federal Republic would have received five votes in the council, whereas the Czech and the Slovak Republics, now that they have "velvetly divorced," might receive eight votes between them in EU-27. By submerging them within the weighted voting of the *colegii* system, these differential advantages would become less significant but not be eliminated altogether.

26. Torsten Peters, "Voting Power after the Enlargement and Options for Decision Making in the European Union," paper presented at the *ECPR Joint Session of Workshops*, Oslo, April 1995. For further discussion of these competing indices of voting power, see Geoffrey Garrett and George Tsebelis, "An Institutional Critique of Intergovernmentalism," *International Organization* 50, no. 2 (Spring 1996): 269–99, and Madeleine Hosli, "Coalitions and Power: Effects of QMV on the Council of the EU," *Journal of Common Market Studies* 34, no. 2 (June 1996): 255–74. As dazzling and "scientific" as these may seem, they are only as good as their initial premises—which, to me, do not seem realistic. Much more promising is the approach taken by Alan Kirman and Mika Widgrén that attempts to put some substantive content into the simulations: "European Economic Decision-making Policy: Progress or Paralysis?" *Economic Policy* 21 (October 1995): 423–60. For a knowledgeable critique of rational choice simplifications applied to council voting, see Hayes-Renshaw and Wallace, "Executive Power in the European Union."

27. Table 4.3 shows the authors' estimated weights. For another estimation, which excludes Malta and Cyprus, see Richard E. Baldwin, *Towards an Integrated Europe* (London: Centre for European Policy Research, 1992), 186–87. Baldwin gives the ten CEECs 47 votes in an EU-25 of 134 votes. The differences seem to be due to the population figures used. For example, if Bulgaria were to reach a population of nine million, it would obtain one more vote in the council. Also, Baldwin is systematically more generous than we are in assigning votes to the three Baltic Republics.

28. One might refer to this as "the (inverted) Lampedusa Ploy" in honor of the author of *Il Gattopardo* who advised his fellow conservative Sicilians that "if

things are going to remain the same around here, they are going to have to change." The trick for the EU, faced with enlargement, will be how to change its decision-making rules so that the present principle of equilibrium by size remains unchanged.

29. As I have noted, there would be no necessity for the *colegii* to meet formally and separately to tally the vote, although it would not be surprising if a certain amount of informal caucusing took place among large, medium, and small countries. It also goes without saying that nothing in this scheme would prevent larger and medium-size countries from seeking to influence the voting of their smaller peers in *Colegii* II or III. What the device does, however, is guarantee the relative bargaining power of the smaller countries in these informal log rolls and trade-offs.

30. Apparently, at the Amsterdam Conference, when the Belgians discovered that according to one of the proposed voting reforms they would have ended up with one less vote than the Dutch, they rejected the prospect out of hand!

31. Votes and seats have been rounded up in all tables. This explains why there are only 85 votes and 624 seats in Table 4.4 and why, in the following tables, the totals do not always add up to 100 (for votes) or 700 (for seats). Also, in the Council of Ministers, when the very smallest countries would be mathematically entitled to less than one-half a vote, their weights have been increased to one.

32. This advantage would not hold true for Luxembourg, whose diminutive size would naturally limit its coalition possibilities.

33. Because of the rounding up of figures, Austria would maintain its four votes. However, given that in future enlargements, Austria would be corrected to three votes and sent down to *Colegio* III, I propose (1) to maintain it in *Colegio* II but decrease its weight to three, (2) send it down to *Colegio* III while maintaining its weight at four, or (3) maintain its four votes and let it stay in *Colegio* II but raise the veto threshold to 31 percent. Any of these three modifications would void the possibility that *Colegio* II alone would be able to veto EU legislation.

34. They might also choose to limit the total number of seats in the European Parliament to, say, seven hundred in order to facilitate discussion and internal procedures. For a similar suggestion, see Mathias Dewatripont et al., *Flexible Integration: Towards a More Effective and Democratic Europe* (London: CEPR, 1995), 172. It should be pointed out that the authors of this collective report were predominantly economists and their concern was much more with effectiveness than democracy.

35. Actually, it would be more democratic to assign votes, seats and *colegio* membership according to the size of their respective citizenries. For most members, this would not change much since the criteria for eligibility for citizenship in Europe are rather standard these days, but it would have the effect of penalizing those countries that discriminate against "denizens" and have in their midst a substantial proportion of residents who are not eligible to vote or stand for office. Countries such as Luxembourg and Switzerland with their mercenary proletariats of "guest workers" and those such as the Baltic Republics that discriminate against resident Russians, Ukrainians, and Belorussians would be especially affected—and for a good democratic reason.

36. It might eventually be necessary to modify this rule if the ministates of Europe become serious about joining the EU. Just imagine the effect of Andorra, Monaco, San Marino, the Vatican, the Isle of Man, the Faeroe Islands, and Liechtenstein on *Colegio* III!

37. Though no exact dates have been given for entry, these four countries are often assumed to be in the best position for early entrance. Since the European Council meeting in Essen in December 1994, all the Central and Eastern European countries (CEECs) enjoying association agreements with the European Union are placed on a "preaccession" path consisting of a "structured dialogue" with the EU, a free trade area, and legal convergence. At the Madrid Meeting of the European Council (December 1995), it was agreed that the fifteen would try to make CEECs' entry negotiations coincide with those dealing with Malta and Cyprus. Thus, the start date would be equal for all and the accession date will depend on economic criteria. The general principles agreed on at the European Council were (1) nondiscrimination, (2) early date for political entry, and (3) long transitional periods. See Commission of the European Communities, European Council, Madrid, December 15 and 16, 1995, *Presidency Conclusions,* (Brussels, December 16, 1995, SI 95 1000).

38. For an imaginative effort at simulating how different structurally determined preferences might affect voting on external trade and budgetary issues in an enlarged EU, see Kirman and Widgrén, "European Economic Decision-making Policy."

39. Bosnia-Herzegovina has not been included, owing to the difficulty in determining the population and area that might define that polity in the future. Belarus, the Ukraine, Moldova, Russia, and the other former republics and units of the USSR have been considered "beyond the pale" of all possible future Europes. The heads of six center-right or peoples' parties (Belgium, Germany, Ireland, Italy, Luxembourg, and Spain) announced that Turkey would never be admitted to the EU, presumably because of its "Islamic-ness." *Financial Times* (March 5, 1997), p. 2.

5

Why Bother?

The preceding chapters should have convinced the reader that it is neither feasible nor desirable to try to democratize the Euro-polity completely and immediately. Not only would we not know how to do it, but there is also no compelling evidence that Europeans want it. Nothing could be more dangerous for the future of Euro-democracy than to have it thrust upon a citizenry that is not prepared to exercise it and that continues to believe its interests and passions are best defended by *national,* not supranational, democracy.

However, I hope the arguments in the preceding chapters will have convinced the reader that it is possible and may even be timely to begin to improve the quality of Euro-democracy through some modest reforms in the way citizenship, representation, and decision making are practiced within the institutions of the European Union. Manifestly, I have not been able to offer a comprehensive vision of what the end product will look like, but specific and incremental steps could be taken to supplement (and not supplant) the mechanisms of accountability that presently exist within its member states.

If my initial hunch was correct—that the rules and practices of an eventual Euro-democracy will have to be quite different from those existing at the national level—then it is all the more imperative that Europeans act cautiously when experimenting with political arrangements whose configuration will be unprecedented and whose consequences may prove to be unexpected—even, unfortunate.

TWO REASONS AND AN OPPORTUNITY
SPACE FOR EXPERIMENTATION . . . NOW

In my opinion, it may be timely to begin this experiment with supranational democracy sooner rather than later for two reasons:

1. There is considerable evidence that rules and practices of democracy at the national level have become increasingly contested by citizens. This has not (yet) taken the form of rebellious or even "unconventional" behavior, but of what Gramsci once called "symptoms of morbidity" such as greater electoral abstention, decline in party identification, more frequent turnover in office and rejection of the party in power, lower prestige of politicians and higher unpopularity of chief executives, increased tax evasion, higher rates of litigation against authorities, skyrocketing accusations of official corruption, and, most generally, a widespread impression that contemporary European democracies are simply not working well to protect their citizens. It would be overly dramatic to label this "a general crisis of legitimacy," but something isn't going well—and most national politicians know it.

2. There is even more compelling evidence that individuals and groups within the European Union have become aware of how much its regulations and directives are affecting their daily lives and that they consider these decisions to have been taken in a remote, secretive, unintelligible, and unaccountable fashion. Whatever comfort it may have given them in the past that "unwarranted interference" by the Eurocrats in Brussels could have been vetoed by their respective sovereign national governments, this has been dissipated by the advent of qualified majority voting. Europeans feel themselves, rightly or wrongly, at the mercy of a process of integration that they do not understand and certainly do not control—however much they may enjoy its material benefits. Again, it would be overdramatizing the issue to call this "a crisis of legitimacy," but "permissive consensus" of the past is much less reliable—and supranational officials know it.

These two trends are probably related causally—and together they create a potentially serious "double bind" for the future of democracy in Europe. If the shift of functions to and the increase in supranational authority of the EU have been contributing to decline in the legitimacy of "domestic democracy" by calling into question whether national officials are still capable of responding to the demands of their citizenry, and if the institutions of the EU have yet to acquire a reputation for accountability to these very same citizens when aggregated at the supranational level, then democracy as such in this part of the world could be in jeopardy. Admittedly, the grip of this double bind is still loose but tightening.[1] The national "morbidity symptoms" show no sign of abating; the supranational "permissive consensus" shows abundant signs of waning. Between the two, there is still space for the introduction of democratic reforms (which has been a major premise of this book), but who will be willing (and able) to take advantage of the rather unusual political opportunity space formed by monetary unification and eastern enlargement (not to mention, the increasingly skewed outcome of Euro-elections) is by no means clear. The potentiality exists for acting preemptively before the situation reaches a crisis stage and before the compulsion to do something becomes so strong that politicians may overreact, but will it be exploited?

Moreover, if my second hunch is correct, that the "Monnet method" of exploiting the spillovers between functionally related issue arenas to advance the level and scope of integrative institutions has exhausted its potential—precisely because of increased citizen awareness and further politicization—then switching to an overtly political strategy of democratization might be sufficient to renew the momentum that has clearly been lost since the difficult ratification of the Maastricht Treaty and the frustrated expectations of the Amsterdam Treaty. If only one could rekindle within the process of Euro-democratization that same logic of indirection and gradualism based on an underlying structure of functional interdependence and an emerging system of collective problem solving, the process of European integration might be given the *relancement* that it has so frequently sought and so badly needs. Except that this time, the result may not be so foreseeable or controllable. Democratization, especially in such unprecedented circumstances and for such a large-scale polity, is bound to activate unexpected linkages, to involve less predicable publics, and to generate less limited expectations.

INTRODUCING SOME GENERIC
NOTIONS ABOUT DEMOCRATIZATION

We have good reason, thanks to democratic theory, for believing that specific forms of citizenship, representation, and decision making are closely interrelated in a self-reinforcing fashion within stable democratic regimes. But, thanks to the absence of much theorizing about democratization, we are a lot less well informed about how these elements came together historically and even less well informed about how they might combine under contemporary circumstances. The pseudo-subdisciplines of "transitology" and "consolidology" have only just begun to draw attention to these dynamic relations within the neodemocracies of the post-1974 wave of democratization—and it is far from evident that their (tentative) conclusions would have any relevance for democratizing an interstate organization composed not of relatively recent democracies but of relatively ancient ones.[2] About all that we can assert with confidence is that there have been and still are many different sequences involved in the relation between citizenship, representation and decision-making—and that these sequences have produced rather substantial differences in both the rapidity with which democracy was consolidated and the type of democracy that subsequently emerged.

Another thing that we do know is to be wary of reifying the experiences of previous democratizers, especially the experience of a single sequence of nation building, state formation, and regime consolidation. It is very tempting to assert that, because the EU does not have the necessary and sufficient elements that produced democracy in country X, then it cannot possible be democratized. For reasons that are obscure to me, this seems especially characteristic of German scholars who postulate a "universalistic" sequence whereby an *ethnos* must precede a *demos,* and the latter can only be created by an explicit constitutional act whereby this *demos* or people "submits itself to a political order of its own invention."[3] Perhaps this view results from the fact that Germany was one of the few European states where a "belief in communality" (*Gemeinsamkeitsglauben*) preceded the formation of its national state or because of the strength of legal formalism in its juridical tradition (*Verrechtligung*). Elsewhere in Europe, the state was often established long before a "feeling of belonging to a (single) community" existed among its subjects and, indeed, played a significant role in bringing about such a feeling. Moreover, in one major case, there was no single-formal constitutional "act of will," just a lengthy accumulation of precedents (Great Britain). In others (France, Spain, Portugal), there have been so many constitutions and major constitutional revisions that it seems absurd to claim that any of them provided an exclusive foundation for political order. My hunch is that the moment for a dramatic act of "self-constitutionalization" has long since passed in the EU and that the *ethnos-demos-politeia* sequence is going to have to be inverted—or it will not lead to a stable democratic regime within contemporary Europe.

HOW AND WHEN TO CONSTITUTIONALIZE THE EU

A basic presumption of this text has been that the EU at this stage in its development neither needs nor is prepared for a full-scale constitutionalization of its polity. The timing is simply wrong. In the absence of revolution, coup d'état, liberation from foreign occupation, defeat or victory in international war, armed conflict between domestic opponents, sustained mobilization of urban populations against the *ancien régime,* and/or major economic collapse, virtually none of its member states have been able to find the "political opportunity space" for a major overhaul of their ruling institutions.[4] The fact that they all (with one exception) have written constitutions and that this is a presumptive sine qua non for enduring democracy indicate that at some time this issue will have to be tackled—if the EU is ever to be democratized definitively—but not now!

This is not to say that nothing can or should be done in the near future. Certainly, many different drafts of a potential Euro-constitution have been produced, circulated, and promoted. The reason, however, that these efforts have had so little effect may be due less to the quality of the politicolegal talent that went into assembling these impressive documents than to the way in which they were discussed and drafted.

The reigning assumption seems to have been that anything as important as constitutionalizing Europe must be treated as a momentous and concentrated *event,* not a gradual and fitful *process.* Above all, it must be accomplished by experts (constitutional lawyers, for the most part) and protected from the pleading of special interests and the scrutiny of mass publics. Only these specialists can be trusted to produce a coherent and consistent draft that will not reflect the self-serving aims of politicians and their surrounding clienteles.[5]

In my view, this *au-dessus-de-la-mêlée* strategy may have worked relatively well under past circumstances when some type of national emergency or founding moment provided the context for deliberation and choice. It will not produce the same beneficial result in the case of the EU where there is no foreseeable emergency and the founding moment has occurred more than forty years ago.[6] What is needed is an entirely new strategy that adopts a much longer time frame and seeks deliberately to involve special interests and mass publics at various stages of the process. Only by deliberately politicizing the issues involved at the level of Europe as a whole and by gradually building up expectations concerning a more definitive set of rules with regard to citizenship, representation, and decision making can one imagine a successful constitutionalization of the EU. Admittedly, this is not the way most of the member states went about accomplishing this task, but as we have already seen, the EU is not a mere repetition of previous nation-, state-, and regime-building processes, and it may well be leading to an outcome that is unprecedented.[7]

The starting point would be to acknowledge that it is by no means clear whether the EU should be constitutionalized now and, if so, how this should be accomplished. Constitutional lawyers and federalists obviously are trained to think that such a signed, sealed, and ratified document is essential for the promotion of an orderly political process, and the sooner this is done the better. But the EU has not been functioning so badly with its pastiche of treaties converted into a quasi-constitution.[8] Moreover, as the circulated drafts testify, these specialists are not in agreement. Each has his or her preferred format based on perceptions of previous performance at the national level in Europe and North America. These range from a loosely linked confederation to a tightly coordinated federation—and include all the intermediate points along this continuum. But as a scholarly collectivity, they have no reason to be confident that any of these formats will have the same (presumably beneficial) impact when applied to the supranational level. The massive shift in scale, the greater heterogeneity of identities and interests, the wider range of development levels, and, most of all, the unprecedented process of gradual and voluntary polity formation all conspire to make the contemporary outcome of a constitutionalized Euro-polity much less predictable than the earlier national efforts.

AN INITIAL REFERENDUM

Once one admits the intrinsic uncertainty and unpredictability involved in the effort to constitutionalize the EU, the answer becomes obvious: turn to the citizens of Europe in their collective wisdom and try to ascertain what their expectations and assumptions may be. This is *not* a populist appeal that presumes that "the people" (there is no such thing in Europe) are united, know what they want, and can be counted on to produce their own constitution by some process of massive deliberation. It is simply a prudential observation that, especially when experts manifestly do not know what their clients want or what to do in order to satisfy those desires, it makes good political sense not to move too far ahead of them and to initiate a gradual effort aimed at getting Euro-citizens to think about the metarules that should eventually govern the accountability of their rulers—*before* a crisis emerges that will force them to act more hurriedly and less reflexively. No doubt that the first returns from such a popular consultation will be confused and very disparate from one country/region to another, but considered as a process that might take twelve to fifteen years, the effort may well be worthwhile. Moreover, if it is done in a specifically "open-ended" fashion, the information gathered should be invaluable in crafting a flexible and asymmetrical institutional format that fits the emerging Euro-polity much better than the more classic federal or confederal ones.

I propose that the European citizenry on the occasion of a referendum attached to one of its regular elections for the European Parliament be asked the following tripartite question:[9]

Should the deputies chosen on . . . (a specific date, not the present one, but that of a forthcoming election to the European Parliament) form a constituent assembly to draft a democratic constitution for the European Union?

Choose one from the three alternatives below:

1. No, the existing institutions of the EU should only be modified by treaties that have been negotiated and ratified unanimously by its sovereign member states.
2. Yes, but the constituent assembly should devote its primary effort to limiting the powers of the EU and to ensuring the continued sovereignty of its member states.
3. Yes, and the constituent assembly should produce a draft designed to make the institutions of the EU capable of acting effectively in the interests of Europe as a whole, even if that means reducing the sovereignty of its member states.

The wording is a bit rough, but the reader will have grasped the intent. Euro-citizens would be offered a genuine metapolicy choice—the outcome of which, as far as I can judge, would be quite uncertain. It might even have to be repeated several times before a clear majority preferred the latter two, positive options. Until such a relative consensus exists in the public at large, however, I am convinced that all efforts at constitutionalization by select groups of politicians or experts will be fruitless. What is especially important is that Euro-citizens be made aware sufficiently in advance (i.e., five years before its convocation) that such a possibility exists and that it be made clear to them that the constitutionalizing process will be a genuinely open and competitive one. This means overcoming the intrinsic bias in "normal" Euro-elections to produce an assembly whose preferences are considerably more "federal" than those of the population at large. Admittedly the low (and declining) turnout for Euro-elections does present a problem of self-selectivity; nevertheless, one could legitimately expect that the prospect of a constituent assembly based on rival conceptions of the future Euro-polity would be a sufficient incentive to convince Euro-skeptics and even Euro-phobes to participate. The result should be an assembly of representatives that better reflects the full range of citizen preferences—and, incidentally, will have contributed significantly to the creation of a distinctive "European public sphere" in the course of its convocation.

The decision rule in response to this "nonbinding" referendum would naturally have to be complex and layered (and would have to be clarified in advance). I propose the following guidelines:

1. No official activity involving the drafting of a Euro-constitution would take place until a substantial (61 percent?) proportion of the

voting electorate in a majority of member states approved either item
2 or 3.

2. If, as seems likely, the voting public turns out to be divided between
a "confederal" option limiting EU powers and a "federal" option expanding them, then the subsequent drafting process would have to
involve *two parallel constituent assemblies*—both obviously in contact with each other and sharing substantial portions of the text (say,
on issues of basic rights) but intending to produce alternative texts.

3. The elected deputies would be expected (but not compelled) to follow initially the expressed "mandate" of their respective national or
regional constituency; that is, they would participate in either the
confederal or the federal deliberative process depending on how the
vote went.[10] (Presumably, deputies from constituencies that chose
the first option would initially abstain from participation in either
assembly.)

4. However, once the drafting process had started and deputies had
gained a better understanding of the issues at stake, they would be
permitted to "cross the aisle" but would be individually responsible
for doing so and for justifying their behavior to their constituents.
(Deputies from "no" constituencies could likewise change their
minds and join one of the drafting parties.)

5. Leaving aside the marginal possibility that the two rival assemblies
might converge on a single text, the intermediate product of this no
doubt lengthy and contentious process would be two versions of a
Euro-constitution for subsequent debate and eventual ratification.

6. The Council of Ministers would have to agree unanimously to go
ahead with the rival texts—without necessarily indicating its preference for one or the other. (Presumably with this power to put a halt
to the entire process, the council would be in a position to influence
the deliberations of the European Parliament's two drafting assemblies, and this should contribute to a more evenhanded treatment of
institutional checks and balances than if it were left exclusively in
the hands of parliamentarians.)

7. National (and, in some countries, subnational) parliaments would be
called on to discuss the respective texts and to approve their sub-
mission (without amendment) to the citizenry for definitive ratification. (Presumably, individual deputies and parties would use this occasion to promote one or the other version—or to convince their
followers to reject both.)

What will be crucial to the success of this "constitutionalizing process"
is sustaining over a considerable period of time an exchange with the
Euro-citizenry (or, better, with those segments of it that evince a concern

with how the EU is to be governed). A model for this that would be well worth studying is the recent experience of South Africa. Its constituent assembly met over an entire year in a particularly open and public fashion. Extensive hearings were held; individuals and groups were invited to contact the drafting group by electronic means; a regular newsletter was published and widely circulated; the entire proceedings were extensively covered in the mass media; the ensuing draft was made available (in more than a dozen languages) to all citizens; special efforts were made to use language intelligible to the average person; the final version was ratified only after an intensive process of public justification and debate. If it follows the process proposed here, the EU would have an additional advantage. In the high likelihood that two rival versions of the Euro-constitution will be drafted simultaneously within the same constituent assembly, the flow of information and hence interest in the debate should be enhanced. Citizens and their parties, associations, and movements would be offered competitive projects with which they could identify, and they would more likely feel that their efforts might make a difference.

A SECOND REFERENDUM

The definitive ratification of the Euro-constitution would involve a second Europe-wide referendum—to be held simultaneously and identically in all member states—at which Euro-citizens would be asked to choose between the two texts (or to reject both).

At this point, a very complex situation could arise, and it is precisely this prospect that may encourage greater cooperation (which is not to say collusion) among the drafters. The Euro-electorate could reject both the confederal and federal texts, although this seems unlikely given both the previous consultation at the initiation of the process and the institutional investment subsequently involved. A clear majority of the citizenry in virtually all member states could approve one or the other of the texts. This seems much less likely to me—barring some unforeseeable convergence of opinion among national and subnational publics that have, so far, expressed quite divergent preferences with regard to EU institutions (as well as policies). So, we are led to the (tentative) conclusion that the "confederal" version will prevail in some countries and the "federal" one in others—perhaps with some even opting for no constitution at all! Confusing as it may sound, such an outcome would be an accurate reflection of the "diversity in unity" that is such a major element in Europe's political reality.

The question is what to do "constitutionally" in the face of this divided outcome. Giving up altogether would make a mockery of all the preceding effort; going ahead by installing the version that gathered the most support would override a (presumably) sizable minority.[11]

The unorthodox but nonetheless appropriate response might well be to go ahead with both! No doubt this is a horrifying thought to juridical purists, but perhaps a viable concession to the diversity embedded in European society. Suppose for a minute that both constitutions would share two elements: (1) a joint definition of accountability in terms of basic democratic principles and (2) a minimum common denominator in terms of substantive policies. These would constitute a dual *acquis communautaire* that all present and future members of the EU agree to respect. They would then be free to differ primarily along the following lines:

1. *Irrevocability:* To be credible, the "federal" version would have to commit its member states (and their subunits) to a permanent arrangement without any foreseeable dissolution, whereas the "confederal" charter is likely to contain the explicit right to independent withdrawal.[12]

2. *Compétences:* In the weaker document, the "subsidiary" powers of the central government would be explicitly limited to a predetermined list and all remaining powers would be exclusively assigned to the member states or their subunits; in the stronger version, not only would the list of exclusive federal *compétences* be more extensive, but it would also be easier to extend it should the functional necessity arise. Both documents might contain provisions for so-called "shared" or "overlapping" powers, as well as for the establishment of independent regulatory commissions. The former is more characteristic of "cooperative federalism," the latter of a more centralized version.

3. *Decision rules:* Presumably, the federal version would rely more extensively on weighted or simple majority principles; the confederal one would stress the need for higher thresholds, even for unanimity on certain issues. Needless to say, the respective roles of the Council of Ministers, the commission, and the parliament (or their successors) could be expected to differ considerably—although both versions would contain more or less the same institutions and rules for admission to them. Both are also likely to share an emphasis on the participation of governments of member states (as in Germany and Switzerland), rather than individual citizens grouped according to territorial constituencies (as in the United States).

4. *Asymmetries:* Should the stronger draft follow the classic federalist formula, the emphasis would be on the uniformity of rights and obligations for all participating individuals and collectivities; the weaker version might well include provisions for differential (as well as deferred) forms of participation.

These do not seem (to me) to be radically divergent principles, and they should be compatible within the same polity. One subset of members—those in which the confederal alternative prevailed—would be bound by a different, less constraining set of rules than would those whose citizenries had chosen the federal one. Europe would find itself with a "core area" that was prepared to move ahead further and faster toward political integration and a "periphery" that accepted a common *acquis communautaire* but was unwilling to extend for the foreseeable future.[13] Needless to say, the latter countries would have the right—once they had experienced the consequences of peripheral status—to join the former, but only once they had gone through all the formalities of intergovernmental negotiation and ratification via popular referendum. Those countries (and their populations) that initially chose the federal option could, however, change their political status only under quite exceptional conditions.

I admit that designing a polity whose members would be subject to two different constitutions (even if the one were to be firmly embedded within the other) does not sound like an ideal state of affairs. Some parallels do exist (e.g., the status of self-governing Native American tribes within the United States, that of the so-called "historical regions" in Spain, or that claimed by Quebec within the Canadian Federation), and both systems would be inserted with the same overriding judicial procedure for resolving eventual conflicts (presuming the comprehensive justiciability of the ECJ). Nevertheless, the best one could claim is that such a flexible formula does correspond to the reality of contemporary Europe (and even more to an EU that has expanded to more than twenty members) and that it might just prove to be a temporary expedient.

SOME MOTIVES FOR URGENCY

But why bother? And, especially, why bother to act now? After all, there is (presumptively) monetary unification in Europe's near future. Will it not generate lots of spillover effects and thereby provide the process of economic integration with a renewed momentum? Why not wait until things get worse and then—as the pro-integration forces have done several times in the past—exploit the contradictions to push the process further? Preemption is hardly the most compelling of motives in politics, and certainly not one of the noblest.

And how do we know, anyway, that the EU is bound for such a crisis? Maybe it is time to call a halt to all this business of further European integration. Why not leave well enough alone and simply consolidate the present gains of regional free trade and factor mobility? Why not leave what remains of market regulation, welfare provision, and security protection to national polities that have (presumably) been strengthened by the process and that (demonstrably) still have a predominant claim on the loyalty of their citizens? And even if there are some areas of positive policy making that must remain Europeanized, why not just strengthen national democratic processes to monitor and control them?

So, why bother with this much riskier process of European political integration via democratization? Might it not produce a contrary effect, that is, even greater resistance to cooperative policy making and the further "pooling" of national sovereignties? Worse yet, might it not just trigger an increase in expectations on the part of newly empowered Euro-citizens, a proliferation of channels for Euro-representation that will just confuse those who attempt to use them, and the establishment of new decision-making procedures for Euro-agencies that are even more bureaucratic, remote, and alienating than the national ones they are displacing?

These are all serious queries. Any eventual serious effort at Euro-democratization would have to cope with them and provide convincing counterarguments. I, alas, do not have answers for all of them, and the answers I do have are more in the nature of impressionistically compiled "hunches" than scientifically confirmed "observations":

- Monetary unification, if and when it occurs, will be so contained institutionally and so confined functionally that it will not have the same potentiality for generating spillover as did policy expansions in the past.
- Even so, the politicization of mass publics at the national level will make it increasingly difficult for technocrats and organized interests to exploit its side effects without resistance.
- The process of economic integration cannot be stopped at will; least of all, it cannot be confined to the status of a mere free trade area without jeopardizing the *acquis communautaire* that is essential for sustaining the political consensus and economic rules that reproduce that market.
- Moreover, if that *acquis* of consensus on rules and substantive distributions is significantly threatened, so will be the very institutions of the EU, and that will eventually force the member states to revise their general policy in Europe, which could even jeopardize its status as a "security community."
- The mere prospect of endangering Europe's security community (i.e., the shared faith that force will not be used, under any circumstances to resolve disputes between states) would so risk undermining the interests of all EU member states that they will do (almost) anything to prevent it.

- National states and their political processes—pace the protestations of such scholars as Donald Puchala, Alan Milward, and Andrew Moravscik—have not been strengthened by the process of European integration (whatever their intentions); hence, they have irretrievably lost the capacity to act autonomously and effectively in many policy areas—even if the EU should disappear altogether.
- National citizens are sufficiently aware of this and the costs involved in returning to the *statu quo ante* so that only a minority would be willing to pay the price for such a retrenchment. Most would support a further enlargement of EU *compétences* rather than risk the collapse of the *acquis* and even more, the security community behind it.
- Regardless of how national citizens might divide on this issue—and even more if they are seriously divided on it—it is not conceivable that their collective efforts at the national level alone would be sufficient to ensure the accountability of supranational authorities, without significant changes in the rules of EU citizenship, representation, and decision making.
- Finally, it will be virtually impossible for national or supranational actors to do nothing about existing EU decision-making rules since the admission of, at least, some of the Eastern European countries cannot be avoided in the near future, which is bound to put an unbearable strain on these rules—not to mention on existing distributions of benefits.

*   *   *

I began this book with several general assumptions that I thought were plausible. I have concluded it with several, more specific assertions that I admit are more speculative. Hopefully, between these two extremes, the reader will have gleaned something useful or at least thought-provoking about the prospective democratization of the European Union.

AN EXCURSUS ON THE PROBLEM OF AGENCY

So far, I have studiously avoided the delicate issue of what agent (or, better, what coalition of agents) might bring about these reforms—however modest—in the nature of EU institutions. I have hinted, occasionally, at who should not do it. For example, I expressed skepticism about the wisdom of the European Parliament's drafting new constitutions whose main purpose would be to increase its own powers. I have repeatedly observed that there is no attitudinal or behavioral evidence of a substantial "democracy deficit"; therefore, there is neither the awareness of imminent crisis among elites nor the prospective of a spontaneous mobilization among masses that might provide a sense of urgency for the reform process. There are, however, enough "morbidity symptoms" surrounding the institutions of the EU to convince actors that they cannot continue forever with the same practices and that at some point they will have to take seriously the notion that the rules will have to be changed.

Clouding the whole issue is the ambiguous role of so-called historical agents. The process of European integration has tended to cut across the classes, sectors, regions, professions, cultures, and religions that were formed by previous processes of societal development, state formation, and regime consolidation. Its relative winners and losers do not coincide neatly with these preestablished lines of cleavage (which, as we have seen, is one of the reasons that the emerging Euro-party system is so unlikely to replicate national ones). Some workers, farmers, professionals, persons in peripheral locations, members of religious denominations, and others have done well; others less well; relatively few have suffered absolutely. Regardless of the distribution, however, the net impact has rarely been cumulative (i.e., aligned with previous sources of discrimination and inequality).

Most important, it has yet to reproduce a polarized pattern of conflict, although there are signs that a loose coalition of losers is forming and mobilizing around issues that, ironically, the EU has little power to resolve but can easily be blamed for exacerbating: foreign migration, "ghettoization," racial intolerance, religious fundamentalism, ethical laxity, persistent unemployment, and, of course, all the nefarious effects of globalization. Unfortunately from the perspective of agency, this anti-integration group is not yet sufficiently threatening to provoke a pro-integration response in favor of reform, but it is growing in importance and could even hold the crucial balance in a few national polities.

There is one historical agent that has definitely been strengthened by the EU and that would have the capacity to press for reform if the integration process were to be significantly threatened. That group is the European bourgeoisie. Granted that its members—especially those in small and medium-size enterprises—have not benefited uniformly, granted that some of the very largest ones may be more concerned with global rather than regional prospects and granted that many of its members are not European by nationality; nevertheless, most of them stand to lose a great deal if the EU were to decline markedly in legitimacy and decision-making capacity. Unfortunately, this bourgeoisie and its middle-class allies have not been sufficiently challenged. Ideologically, its "liberal" positions have never been more dominant; practically, its "natural" opponent, the organized working class, has been weakened. If and when the anti-EU forces do pose a threat, this bourgeoisie may be much more likely to seek retrenchment behind a phalanx of technocrats than to take the risk of opening up the process to the uncertainties of transparency, popular participation, mass party competition, citizen accountability, and redistributive demands. The national bourgeoisies eventually (and reluctantly) went along with such a project in their respective national states under social and cultural conditions that favored their hegemony. The present moment certainly favors a repetition of such a calculus in that the owners of productive property would seem to have little to fear from their employees and workers and the complex rules of the game make it exceedingly difficult for a radical majority to change the existing distribution of wealth.[14] Nevertheless, the sheer scale of the effort at democratizing the Euro-polity, plus the presence in it of social and economic groups with different expectations and traditions of class conflict, could make even the most "triumphant" Euro-bourgeoisie reluctant to take on the risk.

To the extent that eventual democratization comes about by stealth, via piecemeal reforms and indirect measures, the need for a coherent agent is considerably diminished. Depending on the pace and sequence of these changes in the rules, each one of them may only require a "local" majority—however weighted and combined. Some of the measures that I proposed were so modest that they might be implemented by simple majority within the existing framework of treaties. Others would, no doubt, require a qualified majority or even unanimity in the Council of Ministers and codecision with the parliament. A few would have to travel the entire "treaty route" of approval by national parliaments in all member states and even ratification by popular referenda in a few cases.

In this event, they might be helped by what is one of the major ironies of the integration process at its present stage. The politicization that has occurred during the past decade has taken a quite unanticipated form. National politicians—presumably, the elite most sensitive to issues of national sovereignty and anxious to conserve it—have repeatedly supported major extensions of the scope and level of EU authority (with the notable exception of the British Conservatives); national citizens—presumably, the group most benefited from the facilitations and subsidies of EU policies—have consistently proven reluctant to approve these extensions (when they have been given an opportunity to do so). In other words, for relatively piecemeal reforms, there does not seem to be an agency problem on the side of most governing national elites. Either they understand the futility of pretending to exert national sovereignty, or they are convinced of the desirability of a supranational response. The problem lies in convincing mass publics to go along. Now, since future democratic reforms such as I have proposed are intended precisely to bring these publics into a closer and more responsible relation to the integration process, then it should be much easier to convince them that it is in their interest and that of the EU as a whole to approve these initiatives. Moreover, once they have been approved by the full treaty ratification process, these rules will be much more difficult to change or abrogate than would be the case with an ordinary constitution, since this would require the unanimous consent of all other members for the ratification of another treaty!

NOTES

1. Presumably, something like this double bind is what Fritz Scharpf had in mind when he wrote, "Since . . . Europe is part of the problem (of democratic legitimacy), European policies can also help alleviate it." "Governing in Europe: Effective and Democratic," unpublished paper, Max Planck Institute for the Study of Societies, Cologne, no date, 8.

2. Guillermo O'Donnell and Philippe C. Schmitter, *Transitions from Authoritarian Rule: Prospects for Democracy: Tentative Conclusions about Uncertain Democracies* (Baltimore, Md.: Johns Hopkins University Press, 1986). Also, Philippe C. Schmitter, "Transitology: The Science or the Art of Democratization?" in *The Consolidation of Democracy in Latin America,* ed. Joseph Tulchin (Boulder, Colo.: Rienner, 1995), 11–44.

3. The quote is from Claus Offe, "The Democratic Welfare State: A European Regime under the Strain of European Integration" (Humboldt University, unpublished essay, 1999), but it seems reflective of a broader strand of German thinking that goes back to Jellinek, Weber, Habermas, and the contemporary German Supreme Court judge, Dieter Grimm—all of whom are cited approvingly.

4. I can only think of one clear case: Switzerland in the early 1870s. It would be interesting to explore this exception, although the fact that this country had a "one-party-dominant-system" (*Freisinnige/Radical*) at the time must have been an important factor—and not one that can be repeated at the EU level.

5. The fact that several of these constitutional drafts have come out of the European Parliament and that one of their most manifest objectives was to increase the powers of that very same institution suggests that "institutional"—if not "personal"—self-interest cannot be ruled out of the process.

6. The various and sundry "crises" that are likely to be generated by eastern enlargement, as well as by politicization at the national level and implementation deficits at the European level, are better addressed by episodic intergovernmental negotiations and the sort of "modest reforms" of existing institutions that were discussed in chapters 2 to 4.

7. In other words, I emphatically disagree with the conclusion of Fritz Scharpf that "the [EU's] democracy deficit cannot be reformed away." "Democratic Policy in Europe," in *The European Yearbook of Comparative Government and Public Administration* (Baden-Baden: Nomos, and Boulder, Colo.: Westview), ed. J. J. Hesse and T. A. J. Toonen, vol. 2/1995, 91. In my view, it can only be reformed away and any effort to resolve it in the near future by full-scale constitutionalization will only be counter1productive.

8. On this issue of the EU treaties as "quasi-constitutions," see J. H. Weiler, "The Transformation of Europe," *Yale Law Journal* 100 (1991): 2403–83, and "European Neo-Constitutionalism: In Search of Foundations for the European Constitutional Order," *Political Studies* 44 (1996): 517–33.

9. One minor problem has been resolved. Great Britain, until the last Euro-election, used a first-past-the-post, simple majoritarian system for electing its Euro-deputies. Nothing could have been less appropriate for a constituent assembly in which it is especially important that the widest possible range of political

preferences be included in the deliberations. The ideal system (as was discussed briefly in chap. 3) would be proportional representation based on closed lists (to improve the prospects for intraparty discipline) for subnational constituencies—at least in the larger countries and in those with significant regional disparities or identities. With two exceptions (France and Spain, which still use single national lists), this system now prevails where it is most needed.

10. One possible objection to this "assignment principle" could well be that the results across constituencies within the same country will tend to differ *within* and not just *between* existing political parties. Indeed, given the internal divisions that can already be observed over much less significant issues, one can imagine that Euro-deputies are quite likely to be elected under the same party label by voters who have revealed their preference for quite different types of Euro-polity—or even for no constitutionalized Euro-polity at all. Much as this might make national party politicians wary of offering their followers such a potentially divisive opportunity, it does offer a splendid opportunity for the structuration of a genuinely European party system. The two drafting committees—the confederals and the federals—could well be the prototypes of future bipolarized competition at the supranational level.

11. As the example of the Basque response to the 1975 Spanish constitution demonstrates, even a minority within a minority region can use its rejection of a constitution that was otherwise massively approved by the electorate to question the legitimacy of the document and even to justify armed resistance to the regime it empowers.

12. This raises the issue of the unit that should have the right to withdraw from a confederal arrangement. Extreme liberal versions would allow not only member states to do so but also any of their subunits with more than ten million inhabitants! Frank Vibert, "A Proposal for a European Constitution," in *The European Yearbook of Comparative Government and Public Administration,* ed. J. J. Hesse and T. A. J. Toonen, vol. 1 (1995), 285–97. Heidrun Abromeit would even permit "sectoral defections," if ratified by referendum. *Democracy in Europe: Legitimising Politics in a Nonstate Polity* (New York: Berghan, 1998). Needless to say, both proposals face serious difficulties in defining the appropriate universe of application. Would any city of ten million be eligible? Would any social group of ten million be eligible regardless of where it lived? Do producers of San Marzano tomatoes constitute a different sector from those producing another variety? Also, if the withdrawal were unilateral and based on a single referendum, would it not be exploited opportunistically as an omnipresent threat that could be wielded simply in order to bargain for better exemptions or subsidies?

13. The viability of such a "dual" polity would depend to some degree on *where* and not just *whether* such a center-periphery split developed. Hopefully, the federalists would be concentrated in a contiguous core area—more or less coincident with the original six—and the confederalists would find themselves on the northern, southern, and eastern frontiers. Gradually and voluntarily, the outer layers could be expected to join the core (with the likely exception of Switzerland, which, for the foreseeable future, seems likely to retain its status as "the hole in the European doughnut.")

14. There is one additional favorable feature. To the extent that the coalition opposing European integration comes to resemble more and more the coalition of losers that provided mass support for fascism and national socialism, the Euro-bourgeoisie will have much more of an incentive to oppose it. Various national bourgeoisies made the historical mistake of backing these movements as a *moindre mal* against communism and socialism in the 1920s and 1930s—and barely survived to acknowledge their mistake.

Bibliography

Abromeit, Heidrun. *Democracy in Europe: Legitimising Politics in a Nonstate Polity.* New York: Berghan, 1998.

Apter, David. *Ghana in Transition.* New York: Atheneum, 1963.

Baldwin, Richard E. *Towards an Integrated Europe.* London: Centre for European Policy Research, 1992.

Barber, Lionel. "The Men Who Run Europe." *Financial Times,* March 11–12, 1995.

Berten, André. "Identité européenne, une ou multiple?" in *L'Europe au soir du siècle: Identité et démocratie,* ed. Jacques Lenoble and Nicole Dewandre. Paris: Esprit, 1992.

Brubaker, Roger. "Traditions of Nationhood and Politics of Citizenship." Social Science Research Council (New York), *States and Social Structures Newsletter* 9 (Winter 1989): 4–8.

Calhoun, John C. *A Disquisition on Government.* New York: Peter Smith, 1943 (originally published in 1853).

Caporaso, James A. *The Structure and Function of European Integration.* Pacific Palisades, Calif.: Goodyear, 1974.

Castiglione, Dario. "Contracts and Constitutions," in *Democracy and Constitutional Culture in the Union of Europe,* ed. R. Bellamy, V. Bufacchi, and D. Castiglione. London: Lothian Foundation Press, 1995.

Castro Oliveira, Alvaro. "Resident Third Country Nationals: Is It Too Early to Grant Them Union Citizenship?" paper presented at the EUI, European Forum Conference on European Citizenship: An Institutional Challenge, Florence, June 13–15, 1996.

Commission of the European Communities, European Council—Madrid, December 15 and 16, 1995. *Presidency Conclusions* (Brussels: December 16, 1995, SI 95 1000).

Dahl, Robert A. *After the Revolution: Authority in a Good Society.* New Haven, Conn.: Yale University Press, 1970.

——. *Democracy and Its Critics.* New Haven, Conn.: Yale University Press, 1989.

Dahrendorf, Ralf. "Citizenship and Beyond: The Social Dynamics of an Idea." *Social Research* 41, no. 4 (Winter 1974).

Deutsch, Karl, et al. *Political Community and the North Atlantic Area.* Princeton, N.J.: Princeton University Press, 1957.

Dewatripont, Mathias, et al. *Flexible Integration: Towards a More Effective and Democratic Europe.* London: Centre for European Policy Research, 1995.

Di Palma, Giuseppe. *Surviving without Governing.* Berkeley: University of California Press, 1977.

Earnshaw, David, and David Judge. "The European Parliament and the Sweeteners Directive: From Footnote to Inter-Institutional Conflict." *Journal of Common Market Studies* 31, no. 1 (March 1993): 103–16.

Economic and Social Committee of the European Communities, *Community Advisory Committees for the Representation of Socio-Economic Interests*, Farnborough: Saxon, 1980.

European Commission. *Report on the Operation of the Treaty of European Union.* SEC(95), 731, May 10, 1995.

European Council. *Bulletin EC* 10-1992, pt. I.8, p. 9.

Falkner Gerda, and Michael Nentwich. *European Union: Democratic Perspectives after 1996.* Vienna: Service Fachverlang, 1995.

Ferry, Jean-Marc. "Identité et citoyenneté européennes," in *L'Europe au soir du siècle: Identité et démocratie*, ed. Jacques Lenoble and Nicole Dewandre. Paris: Esprit, 1992.

Ferry, Jean-Marc, and Paul Thibaud. *Discussion sur l'Europe.* Paris: Calmann-Lévy, 1992.

Garrett, Geoffrey, and George Tsebelis. "An Institutional Critique of Intergovernmentalism." *International Organization* 50, no. 2 (Spring 1996): 269–99.

Greenwood, J., and K. Ronit. "Interest Groups in the European Community: Newly Emerging Dynamics and Forms." *Western European Politics* 17, no. 1 (January 1994): 31–52.

Groot, Gérard-René de. "The Relationship between the Nationality of the Member-States of the European Union and European Citizenship," paper presented at the EUI European Forum Conference on European Citizenship: An Institutional Challenge, Florence, June 13–15, 1996.

Gross, Andreas. "Zwölf Denkantösse für ein (direkt-) demokratisch verfaßtes Europa," in *Mehr Demokratie für Europa: Ideen und Ansätze*, ed. Menno Wolters et al. Bonn: Stiftung Mitarbeit, 1994.

Haas, Ernst B. *The Uniting of Europe.* Stanford, Calif.: Stanford University Press, 1958.

Habermas, Jürgen. *Strukturwandel der Öffentlichkeit.* Frankfurt: Suhrkamp, 1990.

——. "Citizenship and National Identity: Some Reflections on the Future of Europe," in *Theorizing Citizenship*, ed. Ronald Beiner. Albany: State University of New York Press, 1995.

Hayes-Renshaw, Fiona, and Helen Wallace. "Executive Power in the European Union: The Functions and Limits of the Council of Ministers." *Journal of European Public Policy* 2, no. 4 (December 1995): 559–82.

Hosli, Madeleine O. "Coalitions and Power: Effects of QMV on the Council of the EU." *Journal of Common Market Studies* 34, no. 2 (June 1996): 255–73.

——. "Admission of European Free Trade Association States to the European Community: Effects on Voting Power in the European Community Council of Ministers." *International Organization* 47, no. 4 (Autumn 1993): 631.

Kirman, Alan, and Mika Widgrén. "European Economic Decision-making Policy: Progress or Paralysis?" *Economic Policy* 21 (October 1995): 423–60.

Lakeman, Enid. "Elections to the European Parliament, 1989." *Parliamentary Affairs* 43 (January 1990).

Lash, Scott, and John Urry. *The End of Organized Capitalism*. Cambridge: Polity, 1987.

Lijphart, Arend. *Democracies: Patterns of Majoritarian and Consensus Government*. New Haven, Conn.: Yale University Press, 1984.

Lindberg, Leon, and Stuart Scheingold. *Europe's Would-Be Polity*. Upper Saddle River, N.J.: Prentice Hall, 1970.

Lipsius, Justus. "The 1996 IGC." *European Law Review* 20, no. 3 (1995): 235–67.

Lodge, Juliet. "Transparency and Democratic Legitimacy." *Journal of Common Market Studies* 32 (1994): 343–68.

——. "Democracy in the EU: The Interrelationship between Supranational, National and Subnational Levels of Government," in *Démocratie et construction européenne*, ed. Mario Telò. Brussels: Éditions de l'Université de Bruxelles, 1995.

Lodge, Juliet, and V. Herman. *Direct Elections to the European Parliament: A Supranational Perspective*. London: Macmillan, 1982.

Mancini, Federico G. "The Making of a Constitution for Europe," in *The New European Community*, ed. R. Keohane and S. Hoffmann. Boulder, Colo.: Westview, 1991.

Mansbridge, Jane. *Beyond Adversarial Democracy*. New York: Basic Books, 1980.

Marks, Gary, François Nielsen, Leonard Ray, and Jane Salk. "Competencies, Cracks and Conflicts: Regional Mobilization in the European Union," in *Governance in the European Union,* ed. G. Marks et al. London: Sage, 1996.

Marshall, T. H. *Citizenship and Social Class*. Cambridge: Cambridge University Press, 1950.

McLaughlin, Andrew, and Justin Greenwood. "The Management of Interest Representation in the European Union." *Journal of Common Market Studies* 33, no. 1 (March 1995): 143–56.

Middlemas, Keith. *Orchestrating Europe*. London: Fontana, 1995.

Niedermayer, Oskar, and Richard Sinnott, eds. *Public Opinion and Internationalized Governance*. Oxford: Oxford University Press, 1995.

O'Donnell, Guillermo, and Philippe C. Schmitter. *Transitions from Authoritarian Rule: Prospects for Democracy: Tentative Conclusions about Uncertain Democracies.* Baltimore, Md.: Johns Hopkins University Press, 1986.

Offe, Claus. "The Democratic Welfare State: A European Regime under the Strain of European Integration." Humboldt University, unpublished essay, 1999.

Official Journal of the European Communities. No. C 105 of April 13, 1994, and No. C 1 of January 1, 1995.

Olsen, Johan P. *Organized Democracy.* Oslo: Universitetsforlaget, 1983.

Philip, Alan Butt. "Pressure Groups in the European Community." *UACES Occasional Papers* 2 (1985): 45.

Reif, Karl-Heinz. "Nine Second-Order National Elections." *European Journal of Political Research* 8 (1980): 3–45, 145–62.

———. *Ten European Elections.* Aldershot, England: Glower, 1985.

Reif, Karl-Heinz, and Oskar Niedermayer. "The European Parliament and the Political Parties." *Journal of European Integration* 10, nos. 2 and 3 (1987): 157–72.

Rosamund, Ben. "Mapping the European Condition: Theory of Integration and the Integration of Theory." *European Journal of International Relations* 1, no. 3 (September 1995).

Santamaría, Julián, Josep María Renid, and Vicente Cobos. "Los debates sobre el procedimiento electoral uniforme y las caratteristicas diferenciales de las elecciones europeas." *Revista de estudios politicos* 90 (October–December 1995): 11–44.

Scharpf, Fritz. "Democratic Policy in Europe," in *The European Yearbook of Comparative Government and Public Administration*, ed. J. J. Hesse and T. A. J. Toonen, vol. 2. 1995. Baden-Baden: Nomos, and Boulder, Colo.: Westview.

Schattschneider, E. E. *The Semi-Sovereign People.* Hinsdale, Ill.: Dryden, 1975 (originally published in 1960).

Schmitter, Philippe C. "Democratic Theory and Neo-Corporatist Practice." *Social Research* 50, no. 4 (Winter 1983): 885–928.

———. "The Future Euro-Polity and Its Impact upon Private Interest Governance within Member States." *Droit et société* 28 (1994): 659–76.

———. "Interests, Associations and Intermediation in a Reformed Post-Liberal Democracy." *Politische Vierteljahresschrift*, 35, Sonderheft 25, "Staat und Verbaende" (1994): 160–74.

———. "Alternatives for the Future European Polity: Is Federalism the Only Answer?" in *Démocratie et construction européenne*, ed. Mario Telò. Brussels: Editions de l'Université de Bruxelles, 1995.

———. "Transitology: The Science or the Art of Democratization?" in *The Consolidation of Democracy in Latin America*, ed. Joseph Tulchin. Boulder, Colo.: Rienner, 1995.

———. "Examining the Present Euro-Polity with the Help of Past Theories," in *Governance in the European Union*, ed. Gary Marks, Fritz Scharpf, Philippe C. Schmitter and Wolfgang Streeck. London: Sage, 1996.

———. "If the Nation-State Were to Wither Away in Europe, What Might Replace It?" in *The Future of the Nation State*, ed. Svante Gustavsson and Leif Lewin. Stockholm: Nerenius & Santeris and Routledge, 1996.

———. "Imagining the Future of the Euro-Polity with the Help of New Concepts," in *Governance in the European Union*, ed. Gary Marks, Fritz Scharpf, Philippe C. Schmitter and Wolfgang Streeck. London: Sage, 1996.

———. "Exploring the Problematic Triumph of Liberal Democracy and Concluding with a Modest Proposal for Improving Its International Impact," in *Democ-*

racy's Victory and Crisis, ed. Axel Hadénius. Cambridge: Cambridge University Press, 1997.

Schmitter, Philippe C., and Terry Karl. "What Democracy Is . . . and Is Not." *Journal of Democracy* 2, no. 3 (Summer 1991): 75–88.

——. "The Types of Democracy Emerging in Southern and Eastern Europe and South and Central America," in *Bound to Change: Consolidating Democracy in Central Europe*, ed. Peter Volten. New York: Institute for East-West Security Studies, 1992.

Schmitter, Philippe C., and Wolfgang Streeck. "Organized Interests and the Europe of 1992," in *Political Power and Social Change: The United States Faces the United Europe*, ed. N. J. Ornstein and M. Perlman. Washington, D.C.: AEI Press, 1991.

Sidjanski, Dusan, and Ural Ayberk. "Le Nouveau visage des groupes d'intérêt communautaires." *Revue d'intégration européenne* 10 (Winter-Spring 1987): 173–201.

Sinnott, Richard, and N. Winston. "Disintegrative Tendencies in EU Public Opinion." Paper for the ECPR Joint Sessions, Oslo, 1996.

Streeck, Wolfgang, and Philippe C. Schmitter. "From National Corporatism to Transnational Pluralism: Organized Interests in the Single European Market." *Politics & Society* 19, no. 2 (June 1991): 133–64.

Torsten, Peters. "Voting Power after the Enlargement and Options for Decision Making in the European Union," paper presented at the ECPR Joint Session of Workshops, Oslo, April 1995.

Traxler, Franz, and Philippe C. Schmitter. "Perspektiven Europäischer Integration, verbandlicher Interessenintermediation und Politikformulierung," in *Europäische Integration und verbandliche Interessenintermediation*, ed. V. Eichener and H. Voelzkow. Marburg: Metropolis, 1994.

——. "The Emerging Euro-Polity and Organized Interests." *European Journal of International Relations* 1, no. 2 (June 1995): 191–218.

Vibert, Frank. "A Proposal for a European Constitution," in *The European Yearbook of Comparative Government and Public Administration,* ed. J. J. Hesse and T. A. J. Toonen, vol. 1, 285–97. 1994.

Walzer, Michael. *Obligations: Essays on Disobedience, War, and Citizenship*. Cambridge, Mass.: Harvard University Press, 1970.

Weiler, J.-H. "European Neo-Constitutionalism: In Search of Foundations for the European Constitutional Order." *Political Studies* 44 (1996): 517–33.

——. "The Transformation of Europe." *Yale Law Journal* 100 (1991): 2403–83.

Wilson, Frank L. "The Elusive European Party System," paper presented at the ECSA meeting, Charleston, S.C., May 11–14, 1995.

Index

Index of Names

147

About the Author

Philippe C. Schmitter has been on the faculty of the European University Institute (EUI) in Florence since the fall of 1996. He was educated at Dartmouth College, the National Autonomous University of Mexico, and the University of Geneva and received his Ph.D. from the University of California, Berkeley. He taught for many years at the University of Chicago (1967–82) and has been a visiting professor at the University of Brazil in Rio de Janeiro; the Institute for the Integration of Latin America in Buenos Aires, Harvard University; the Universities of Geneva, Zurich, Paris, and Mannheim; the Wissenschaftszentrum in Berlin; the Centro de Estudios Avanzados en Ciencias Sociales in Madrid; the Central European University in Budapest; and the Institut d'Etudes Politiques de Paris. Before coming back to the EUI, he spent the previous ten years as a professor at Stanford University.

Schmitter has conducted research on comparative politics and regional integration in both Latin America and Western Europe, with special emphasis on the politics of organized interests. He is the author of *Interest Conflict and Political Change in Brazil, Autonomy or Dependence as Regional Integration Outcomes: Central America,* and *Military Rule in Latin America* and the coauthor of *Trends toward Corporatist Intermediation* and *Patterns of Corporatist Policy-Making* (both with Gerhard Lehmbruch), *Private Interest Government* (with Wolfgang Streeck), and *Transitions from Authoritarian Rule: Prospects for Democracy,* four volumes (with Guillermo O'Donnell). Currently, he is completing a book on *Essaying the Consolidation of Democracy.*

At Stanford, he served as the director of the Center for European Studies from its foundation in 1986 until early 1992. He has been the recipient of numerous professional awards and fellowships, including a Guggenheim in 1978, and has been vice president of the American Political Science Association.

Professor Schmitter welcomes comments from his readers:

Philippe C. Schmitter
Department of Political and Social Sciences
European University Institute
via dei Roccettini 9
San Domenico di Fiesole (FI)
I-50019 Italia
telephone: 039/55/46 85 274
fax: 039/55/46 85 201
telefonino: 039/338/831 70 73
E-mail: schmitter@datacomm.iue.it

PATRICK MOLINEUX

Hodder & Stoughton

A MEMBER OF THE HODDER HEADLINE GROUP

0340858036   LAN

Dedication

To the memory of Peter Molineux
1931–1999

Orders: please contact Bookpoint Ltd, 130 Milton Park, Abingdon, Oxon OX14 4SB.
Telephone: (44) 01235 827720. Fax: (44) 01235 400454. Lines are open from 9.00–6.00, Monday to Saturday, with a 24-hour message answering service. E-mail address: orders@bookpoint.co.uk

British Library Cataloguing in Publication Data
A catalogue record for this title is available from the British Library.

ISBN 0 340 858036

First published 2002
Impression number   10 9 8 7 6 5 4 3 2 1
Year   2007 2006 2005 2004 2003 2002

Typeset by Servis Filmsetting Ltd, Manchester.
Printed in Great Britain for Hodder & Stoughton Educational, a division of Hodder Headline Plc, 338 Euston Road, London NW1 3BH by J.W. Arrowsmith Ltd, Bristol.

M·C·A
MANAGEMENT
CONSULTANCIES
ASSOCIATION

Series Editor: Fiona Czerniawska, Director of MCA Think Tank.

The MCA was formed in 1956 and represents the leading UK-based consulting firms, which currently employ over 25,000 consultants and generate £4.3bn in annual fee income. The UK consulting industry is worth around £8bn, contributing £1bn to the balance of payments.

As well as setting and maintaining standards in the industry, the MCA supports its member firms with a range of services including events, publications, interest groups and public relations. The Association also works with its members to attract the top talent into the industry. The MCA provides advice on the selection and use of management consultants and is the main source of data on the UK market.

FOR MORE INFORMATION PLEASE CONTACT:
Management Consultancies Association
49 Whitehall
London
SW1A 2BX

Tel: 020 7321 3990
Fax: 020 7321 3991

E-mail: mca@mca.org.uk

www.mca.org.uk